DATA ANALYSIS AND RESEARCH
FOR SPORT AND EXERCISE SCIENCE

Data Analysis and Research for Sport and Exercise Science is a handbook written for undergraduate sport and exercise science students, and will be of particular use to students undertaking quantitative research projects and a research-based dissertation. The book introduces students to the process of conducting independent research in sport and exercise physiology, biomechanics and psychology.

The text is divided into the three main areas of Research Design, Data Analysis and the Interpretation of Findings. Topics covered include:

- Introduction to the scientific research method
- How to conduct a literature review
- How to develop your research question and experimental design
- Using statistical analysis
- Ways to present your data
- Discussing your results and drawing conclusions

Craig Williams is programme director and senior lecturer in sport and exercise science at the University of Exeter. **Chris Wragg** is a lecturer in sport and exercise science at the University of Brighton.

DATA ANALYSIS AND RESEARCH FOR SPORT AND EXERCISE SCIENCE

A student guide

Craig Williams

Chris Wragg

Routledge
Taylor & Francis Group

LONDON AND NEW YORK

First published 2004
by Routledge
2 Park Square, Milton Park, Abingdon, Oxon, OX14 4RN

Simultaneously published in the USA and Canada
by Routledge
270 Madison Ave, New York NY 10016

Routledge is an imprint of the Taylor & Francis Group

Transferred to Digital Printing 2006

© 2004 Craig Williams and Chris Wragg

Typeset in Times by
RefineCatch Limited, Bungay, Suffolk

British Library Cataloguing in Publication Data
A catalogue record for this book is available from the British Library

Library of Congress Cataloging in Publication Data
A catalog record for this book has been requested

ISBN 0–415–28970–X (hbk)
ISBN 0–415–28971–8 (pbk)

Reprinted 2006
Printed and bound by CPI Antony Rowe, Eastbourne

CONTENTS

FIGURES

TABLES

PREFACE

This book is aimed primarily at undergraduate students who are undertaking a dissertation or other independent research project in the field of sport and exercise science. It is designed to be most relevant to quantitative research in this field, which includes physiological, biomechanical and psychological research. It is not our aim to provide you with knowledge relating to these three disciplines, but rather to help you through the process of conducting independent research within them. For undergraduate students, this most commonly takes the form of a dissertation project, and this book is designed to assist students producing a dissertation. However, it will also be relevant to students involved in independent research or study modules.

The book is divided into 3 sections, which relate to different sections of a dissertation. The first section (Chapters 1–3) focuses on principles of scientific study, devising a research question and designing an experiment. This section is most useful when writing the literature review and developing a method for a dissertation. The second section (Chapters 4–7) relates to data analysis and statistical testing and applies directly to the results section of a dissertation. The final section (Chapters 8–10) is centred around interpreting findings and drawing appropriate conclusions, which is obviously critical for the construction of the discussion section of a dissertation. While the book enables students to understand and interpret the results of statistical tests, it is not a statistical software manual. Where necessary reference is made to an appropriate text, in relation to performing statistical tests on SPSS (Coakes and Steed 2001). We have designed this book to be as student-friendly as possible; as a consequence the use of complex statistical formulae has been kept to a minimum, and common, subject-specific examples are used to enhance understanding wherever possible.

The book seeks to provide guidance through the process of conducting independent research, but there is no substitute for the advice and experience of an academic tutor. We advise that this book be used in conjunction with regular tutorials with academic members of staff at your institution.

ACKNOWLEDGEMENTS

We would like thank our colleagues at the University of Exeter and the University of Brighton for their advice and support in the construction of this text. In addition we thank the students on both programmes at these universities for their constant input to our development as educators. We are grateful to SportsDiscus for allowing copyright of material related to sport and exercise science literature. We also acknowledge the important role played initially by Simon Whitmore, and then by Samantha Grant, in providing vital support for the writing process.

Finally we would like to dedicate this book to Caroline and Catherine, without whom life would be impossible.

1

INTRODUCTION TO RESEARCH IN SPORT AND EXERCISE SCIENCE

> We do not think that we know a thing until we are acquainted with its primary conditions or first principles, and have carried our analysis as far as its simplest elements. Plainly therefore in the science of Nature, as in other branches of study, our first task will be to try to determine what relates to its principles.
>
> *Physics* by Aristotle (350 BC)

LEARNING OUTCOMES

Following this chapter you should be able to:

1 identify the concepts that are fundamental to scientific research and distinguish it from other forms of study;
2 outline the separate disciplines within sport and exercise science and explain their interaction within a multidisciplinary and interdisciplinary framework.

Introduction

What is science, and what is scientific research? A fairly obvious question at first glance. The common perception is that science is objective, systematic and involves experimental research. Most people view science as a world of black and white, right and wrong, correct theories and incorrect theories, proof and lack of proof. The stereotype is that you study science if you are meticulous, numerate and lack creativity, and that you study arts if you are flexible, imaginative and wish to make interpretations of your own. Obviously, as scientists you are aware that this picture is inaccurate. If science is black and white, how can you have two pieces of research that each show evidence for theories that oppose one another? Science is so open for interpretation, that it is impossible to say definitively what is science and what is not. For example, does a piece of sports psychology research based upon a questionnaire constitute scientific research? If so, does a structured piece of market research examining consumer behaviour, based upon a questionnaire, constitute scientific research? If so, what about a quest to find your ideal partner through the completion of a questionnaire?

Generally, people have an instinctive sense of what is scientific and what is not, but when it comes to explicitly stating why something is scientific, they are less certain. In order to design good scientific research, it is necessary to understand what science and the scientific process are.

Science is derived from the Latin word *Scientia*, meaning knowledge. However, it has been suggested that it may be traced back to the word *Chyati*, taken from the ancient language of Sanskrit, which was thought to have originated in Northwest India and Pakistan. *Chyati* means to 'cut off', and gives the indication that the earliest understanding of the concept of science may have referred to breaking down understanding to its most fundamental levels, in the sense that we are 'cutting off' areas of knowledge in order to examine their basic principles.

The most common experience of science is of the natural sciences. Natural science relates to the study of the physical world and is usually taken to include physics, biology and chemistry. In a sense these three subjects can be thought of in the same way as the primary colours. All other natural sciences, including exercise physiology and biomechanics, can be thought of as being derived from the three 'primary' sciences. The origins of natural science are located within ancient Greece, and are closely related to the foundation of natural philosophy (see 'The history of science', pp. 2–6). Social science is perhaps the only area of science that exists beyond the boundaries of natural science; however, the history and many of the research principles are shared. Social science, which includes sport and exercise psychology, uses some of the principles of scientific research to study human society, behaviour and individual interaction with society.

The history of science

As previously mentioned, the natural philosophy of ancient Greece is viewed as the starting point for scientific study. A branch of philosophy (*philo* = loving, *sophos* = wise/wisdom), natural philosophy was concerned with the natural world and its processes. Early natural philosophers living around 600–400 BC were predominantly concerned with what things were made of, and how nature was able to transform the condition of everything. Their initial theories centred on different ideas relating to fundamental elements from which everything was comprised. This type of thinking represents a key step in the birth of science, as these early philosophers were starting to try to understand the underlying laws of nature, not through fantastical myths, but through observing natural phenomena.

Logic and deductive reasoning

During these times it was quite common for philosophers to be involved in many aspects of philosophy, not just specialising in this embryonic form of science. Indeed, Aristotle (384–322 BC), in addition to writing on physics and the movement of animals, wrote about dreams, ethics and the Athenian constitution. Aristotle's greatest legacy for science was the concept of logic, described through the collection of works known as the *Organon* (Greek for organ, in this context relating to an instrument of thought). Aristotle's version of logic involved the drawing of a conclusion based upon a combination of observations. One of the main tools of logical inquiry was something referred to as a syllogism. A syllogism is an argument that contains three statements, the first two being premises (NB. not 'premises'), the latter statement being the conclusion. For example, *major premiss*: sport and exercise science students enjoy sport; *minor premiss*: I am a sport and exercise science student; *conclusion*: I enjoy sport.

Aristotle's logic was closely linked to a structured approach to thinking, derived from ancient Greece, called deductive reasoning. This was a process of reasoning that evolved from geometry, where general rules were used to deduce what would occur in specific situations. For instance, given Pythagoras' theorem, the length of the hypotenuse can be predicted, in a specific right-angled triangle, with known side lengths of 3 and 4 cm. This line of deduction was extended to natural philosophy, where conclusions were based upon axioms. An axiom is a generally accepted principle, often considered to be a fundamental truth requiring no proof, such as: 'all animals will eventually die'. The problem with deductive reasoning is that the axioms may be flawed, which will in turn lead to an invalid conclusion. Take, for example, a previously commonly held axiom that heavy objects fall more quickly than light objects. Applying this general principle to the specific situation of an orange and a watermelon dropped from the same height would lead to an incorrect conclusion. While logic and deductive reasoning are problematic because of issues related to the assumptions they make, these approaches heralded the beginning of a system of structured, rational thinking, where conclusions relating to the natural world are based upon theories or principles.

Inductivism

The next critical steps in the development of scientific research methods would not occur until the Renaissance. It is interesting to note that in the time intervening the classical period of history and the Renaissance, modern society owes the continued carrying of the scientific torch to Arabic civilisations. It is easy to forget, with our Eurocentric view of the history of civilisation, that not only was much classical Greek knowledge preserved, but many great advances were made during the Middle Ages by Arabic scholars. Scientists such as Al-Khwarzmi, who made major progress in algebra, and Jabir Ibn Haiyan, who helped to transform the art of alchemy into the scientific discipline of chemistry, were extremely influential in later European scientific development.

Not only did these scholars preserve and advance scientific knowledge within their own civilisations, but the Arabic-inspired collapse of the Byzantine empire is argued to be one of the causes of the Renaissance in Europe. The efflux of classically trained scholars from the Byzantine empire – and the preserved classical texts they carried with them (courtesy of Arabic translations) – is viewed as a possible trigger for the suddenly erudite environment in which the Renaissance flourished.

The Renaissance began in Italy during the fourteenth century and spread across Europe during the next two centuries. In this climate of learning, an Englishman, Francis Bacon (1561–1626), emerged as an extremely influential 'Renaissance man' (a term referring to an all-round scholar of this era). Francis Bacon was a politician, a philosopher and a man of literature, but primarily it was to natural science that his most important contributions were made. In 1620 Bacon published his groundbreaking work, which he entitled *Novum Organum* (Latin for 'new organ', relating to a new instrument of thought). Bacon's selection of title was designed to signal his intent that this text should form the basis for a new way of thinking, which should replace the Aristotelian thinking outlined by the much earlier work *Organon*. Further, by choosing to use Latin for his title, rather than Greek, it seems that Bacon was making a statement about his new practical view of science. The Greeks were generally regarded as contemplative, but abstract, whereas the Romans were viewed as being more practical in their application of thinking, as evidenced by their highly developed technology. Francis Bacon believed strongly in a utilitarian application of science. He thought that scientific research would advance human development. His practical approach to scientific thinking was outlined in *Novum Organum*, where he introduced the concept of inductivism. This idea stated that scientific theories and conclusions should not be based on abstract thought and axioms, but rather on actual observations in specific situations. Central to inductivism was the notion of ampliative inference. This involved the application of findings from specific conditions to generate general theories relating to these conditions.

Bacon's approach can be summarised to the following steps:

- Scientists unselectively and objectively collect facts.
- Scientists organise, arrange and classify these facts.
- When scientists have enough facts, they generalise from these facts and create a universal theory.

This approach led to the classical experimental model that still operates today, where scientists set up experiments (specific conditions) and then objectively observe the outcome of experiments. Objectivity was the key to Bacon's approach, where a scientist tried to remove bias exerted by preconceived ideas that they held.

Bacon believed these theories are valid if:

- the number of observations is large;
- observations are taken under a variety of conditions; and
- no observation conflicts with the derived theory.

Around the same time that Francis Bacon was expounding his theories on conducting scientific investigation, a scientist and mathematician was carrying out experiments that exemplified Bacon's ideas. Galileo Galilei (1564–1642) was quickly recognised as a brilliant scholar, being appointed chair of mathematics at the University of Pisa and receiving the backing of the extremely powerful Medici family of Tuscany (demonstrating the importance of funding for scientific research). Galileo also believed in a utilitarian approach to the applications of his research, and developed microscopes, geometrical compasses and a hydraulic pump. However, more importantly, he followed an inductive method of investigation. His theories regarding the mechanics of descent (falling objects), magnetism and astronomy were based upon scientific observation of specific situations. Galileo valued the strength of this form of evidence so greatly that he was prepared to defend the Copernican System of planetary rotation against the doctrine of the Church (potentially a serious crime at the time).

Sir Isaac Newton (1643–1727), the first scientist to be knighted, used an inductive approach to ascend new heights of knowledge. Newton contributed more to natural science than anyone before or since, and his pre-eminent text *Philosophiae Naturalis Principia Mathematica* (abbreviated to *Principia*) is arguably the greatest scientific book ever written. His works on light and colour, universal gravity and the laws of motion were all founded on experimental evidence. Whilst not wishing to temper the brilliance of a scientific legend, it would be biased not to acknowledge how Newton's idiosyncratic response to academic discourse, and his influential position, led to the suppression of notable work from other scientists.

Although in Newton's early career he studied philosophy and chemistry, his later rejection of these two subjects represented an understanding that to research truly a scientific discipline, specialisation was required. This view is summarised by his quote:

> To explain all nature is too difficult a task for any one man or even for any one age. 'Tis much better to do a little with certainty, and leave the rest for others that come after you, than to explain all things.

Newton's decision to leave behind other subjects was symbolic of a schism that occurred within science at around this time, whereby natural science separated into its three primary disciplines, and philosophy was regarded as an entirely separate subject.

Reductionism

In addition to being directed by the inductive approach stemming from Bacon's writings, Sir Isaac Newton was influenced by the writings of another philosopher, René Descartes (1596–1650). Descartes, in his *Rules for the Direction of the Mind* (1625–28), expresses his view that to understand the laws of nature you must first understand the elements that contribute to that law and how they interact. Reductionism, which this approach has come to be known as, essentially states that the whole is equal to the sum of its parts. In understanding these parts in detail, we begin to understand the whole. Descartes' argument is summarised by the following quotes from the *Rules for the Direction of the Mind*: 'it is only concerning genuinely simple and absolute matters that we can have certain knowledge' and 'all human knowledge consists of this one thing, that we perceive distinctly how these simple matters combine to produce other things'.

This way of thinking may seem obvious nowadays, but we must remember that it was opposed to the classical tradition of thought. The classical system of thought, espoused by Aristotle, held that the explanation for a phenomenon was of a higher level than the understanding of each part of the phenomenon. Descartes' rejection of this hierarchical system of thought is epitomised by Newton's quote: 'I keep the subject of my inquiry constantly before me, and wait till the first dawning opens gradually, by little and little, into a full and clear light.' Here, Newton is describing his own reductionist approach to study, where understanding is derived by focusing inquiry on small aspects of the whole.

Antoine Laurent Lavoisier (1743–94), who was born into a wealthy French aristocratic family, provided a stunning example of the application of reductionist thinking. His development of the concept of chemical elements was based upon experiments he performed in his own laboratory, which was funded from the proceeds of his tax-collecting business. His theories, espoused in his book published in 1789, *Elementary Treatise on Chemistry*, reduced every substance into either a pure form of, or some combination of a group of, base substances that cannot be broken down further by chemical means. Unfortunately for Lavoisier, his tax-collecting activities and his aristocratic background meant that the French Revolution, occurring soon after his seminal theories were published, led to his being guillotined in 1794.

Another important example of this approach to scientific investigation is cell theory, first advanced by the German botanist Matthias Jakob Schleiden (1804–81), and the German physiologist Theodor Schwann (1810–82). Following the observations that led to the development of this theory, complex organisms could be viewed as a collection of cells, the future of the whole organism being determined by the properties of the cells.

Descartes had always maintained that scientific evidence, stemming from a reductionist method, was of a higher value than other forms of evidence. The importance of the discoveries that emerged from science, in the centuries following Descartes, consolidated the position that science provided the most significant and influential form of evidence available to European society.

Hypothesis testing

Sir Karl Popper (1902–94) was born in Vienna, and completed his PhD at the University of Vienna in 1928. The Wiener Kreis (Vienna Circle), an influential group of scholars whose members were mathematicians, scientists and philosophers, undoubtedly influenced Popper's early thinking. The activity of the Wiener Kreis represented a re-marriage of science and philosophy, following a period where the two fields had grown increasingly separate. Although Popper later came to criticise the theories generated by the Wiener Kreis, its work gave him his focus and direction, namely the philosophy of science. Through his works *The Logic of Scientific Discovery* and *Conjectures and Refutations*, published in 1934 (translated 1959) and 1963 respectively, Popper advanced a model for scientific investigation that was centred around the testing of hypotheses. These hypotheses refer to statements that are testable through experimentation. He held that the object of scientific inquiry should be to rigorously test a hypothesis. A hypothesis that is found through experimentation to be false may be rejected; a hypothesis that is found not to be false should only be tentatively accepted, as the next experiment or observation may show it to be false. The classic example used to illustrate this is the 'black crow' hypothesis. This states that the hypothesis 'all crows are black', can never be unreservedly accepted, because the next crow observed may be white.

Popper acknowledged that the creation of a hypothesis involved imagination. A scientist devises a hypothesis, not by some perfect process of inductive reasoning, but by using his knowledge and past experience to make an educated guess centred around a plausible theory. It is then the scientist's responsibility to test this hypothesis objectively through experimentation in an attempt to demonstrate that the hypothesis is false. This approach is referred to as the hypothetico-deductive method, because it combines deduction with a structured process of hypothesis testing.

Summary and criticism of the scientific method

There are three main features to the model of inquiry used in contemporary science. These are:

- **Deduction** Evidence is based upon observation in specific situations (often experimental situations).
- **Reductionism** Understanding of a phenomenon is achieved through examination of each underlying element that contributes to the phenomenon.

- **Hypothesis testing** The aim of experimentation is to test a hypothesis objectively and rigorously.

Thomas Kuhn (1922–), and much of the feminist criticism of science related to his work, has questioned the scientific method from a new perspective. Kuhn introduced the notion of the scientific method as a set of beliefs, which he referred to as a paradigm. A community (such as the scientific community) may alter its beliefs slightly in a 'paradigm shift'. This chapter has shown that this has clearly already occurred several times throughout the history of scientific development. The question that is raised is: 'Why should the scientific method be viewed as an infallible approach to discovering knowledge?' This is particularly pertinent given that the scientific community has traditionally represented European males disproportionately in comparison with other demographic groups. Although difficult to answer, this is a question that all practising scientists should always be aware of.

The foundations and development of sport and exercise science

It is difficult to say with any certainty when the birth of sport and exercise science occurred. Prior to sport and exercise science as we know it today, there were different disciplines, which have impacted on its development. These range from subjects in medicine such as anatomy and physiology, psychology, physical education to engineering, statistics and sociology. Sport and exercise science began to emerge after the Second World War and shared some of its roots with the development of physical education (PE). Indeed, many departments in the UK run programmes in physical education alongside those of sport and exercise science. Advances in technology, a greater emphasis on public health and medicine, and an increasing professionalism in sport, have shaped these programmes over the last 50 years to produce today's sport and exercise science. This programme of study is multi-disciplinary, meaning that it shares different perspectives from different disciplines such as physiology, biomechanics, psychology and sociology. As a result, there is a great diversity of research. To try to highlight every contributor to sport and exercise science would be an impossible task and one that would fill many books and not just a single chapter. Therefore, we have tried to select some of the current researchers contributing to the development of sport and exercise science. Inclusion or omission in this brief introduction should not be taken as an indication of the relative importance of scientists in this field, it merely represents a biased viewpoint from the authors' perspectives. To try to contain the extensive amount of material we could have presented, we have delimited this section to three key sub-disciplines, namely biomechanics, physiology and psychology, and to those contributors of the past 50 years.

Professor Neil Armstrong

Neil Armstrong is Professor of Paediatric Physiology at the University of Exeter and is Research Director of the Children's Health and Exercise Research Centre (CHERC), the only specialised laboratory in the United Kingdom dedicated to the study of children's health, exercise and physical activity. He is a former Chairperson of the British Association of Sports Sciences (a forerunner of the British Association of Sport and

Exercise Sciences, BASES). He is a fellow of BASES, the American College of Sports Medicine (ACSM) and the Physical Education Association of the United Kingdom (PEAUK). Neil's research focus is on the aerobic fitness and performance of children, including the effects of growth and maturation on aerobic fitness, physical activity and fitness, and oxygen uptake kinetics in children.

Professor Stuart Biddle

Stuart Biddle is based at Loughborough University and specialises in exercise psychology. Stuart's research specialism includes motivational and emotional aspects of physical activity and exercise. He has edited a text entitled *European Perspectives on Exercise and Sport Psychology* and has also co-edited *Physical Activity and Psychological Well-Being*. He has served as the President of the European Federation of Sport Psychology, and has been Chair of the Scientific Committee of the European College of Sport Science.

Professor Peter Cavanagh

Peter Cavanagh is Professor of Kinesiology, Medicine, Orthopaedics and Rehabilitation, and Biobehavioral Health at the Pennsylvania State University, USA. Peter gained his PhD in Human Biomechanics at the University of London, Royal Free Medical School. He is currently the Director of the Centre for Locomotion Studies and specialises in biomechanical studies of pathological gait, diabetic foot research and management, and reduced-gravity human locomotion. He is an accomplished author of over 100 journals and textbooks. Professor Cavanagh is past Chair of the American Diabetes Association's Foot Council, an honorary member of the American Orthopaedic and Foot Council, past President of the American Society of Biomechanics and the International Society of Biomechanics, and a former trustee of the American College of Sports Medicine. He currently serves on the Science Council of the Universities Space Research Association's (USRA) Division of Space Life Sciences, a US government organisation involved in furthering space science, exploration and education.

Professor Joan Duda

Joan Duda is a Professor of Sports Psychology in the School of Sport and Exercise Sciences at the University of Birmingham. Joan is a past President of the Association for the Advancement of Applied Sport Psychology. She has also served as a committee member on several panels including the North American Society for the Psychology of Sport and Physical Activity, the Sport Psychology Academy, and the International Society for Sport Psychology. She has been awarded fellowship of the Association for the Advancement of Applied Sport Psychology and the American Academy of Kinesiology and Physical Education. Her focus of research is sport motivation and the psychological dimensions of sport and exercise behaviour. She is an author of a text entitled *The Advances in Sport and Exercise Psychology Measurement* (1998).

Professor Roger Enoka

Roger Enoka is Professor of Kinesiology and Applied Physiology at the University of Colorado, USA. He has developed an expertise in the integration of biomechanics and neuromuscular physiology over the last 25 years. He has been funded over the past two years by the National Institute of Health. He is a former President of the American Society of Biomechanics and serves as an advisory panel member of the American Physical Therapy Association and has previously been a section member of the National Institute of Health.

Professor Dan Gould

Dan Gould is a Professor in the Department of Exercise and Sport Science at the University of North Carolina at Greensboro, USA. He has over 20 years' research and experience on the mental attributes of athletic success. He has specifically worked alongside Olympic athletes and using theoretical models applied them to determining successful performance. Much of Dan's expertise focuses on mental training for athletic competition and sport psychology. He has been a consultant for the US Olympic Committee and US Freestyle Ski Team and is co-author of two text books, *Understanding Psychological Preparation for Sport* and *Foundations of Sport and Exercise Psychology*.

Professor Lew Hardy

Lew Hardy is Professor of Health and Human Performance, University of Wales, Bangor. His research areas include stress and performance, group dynamics, processes underlying imagery effects, psychological factors in injury and rehabilitation, goal-setting and motivation. He has worked with several British Olympic sports including gymnastics and is accredited by both BASES and the British Psychological Society. He has co-authored several books including *Understanding Psychological Preparation for Sport: Theory and Practice of Elite Performance*.

Professor Walter Herzog

Walter Herzog is currently a Professor in the Departments of Kinesiology, Mechanical Engineering and Medical Science at the University of Calgary in Canada. He obtained his PhD in Biomechanics at the University of Iowa, USA, in 1985. His research expertise includes basic muscle mechanics and physiology, joint mechanics, biology and injury and the disease processes. His particular, interest is in the external and internal loads impacting on the musculoskeletal system. Previous and current studies include investigations in the adaptive and degenerative responses of muscle, tendon and cartilage, and spinal health. He is a panel member of the Medical Research Council in Canada and is a member of the International Society of Biomechanics, the American Society of Biomechanics and the Canadian Society for Biomechanics.

Professor Paavo Komi

Paavo Komi is a Professor and Head of Department at the University of Jyväskylä in Finland. He specialises in muscle research in relation to neuromuscular factors, endurance and sprint adaptations. He is an honorary member of the International Council of Sport Science and Physical Education (ICSSPE) as well as a former President of the European College of Sport Science (ECSS). He is a recipient of a fellowship from the American College of Sports Medicine (ACSM) and is a member of the Medical Commission of the International Olympic Committee.

Professor Ron Maughan

Ron Maughan is based at Loughborough University and specialises in nutrition and environmental physiology, investigating such factors as hydration strategies and the effects of heat. He is a member of the British Olympic Medical Commission with responsibility for the organisation of sports science support to British Olympians. He is a regular contributor to journals, magazines and sport associations on dehydration and nutrition and has recently performed scientific studies related to the effects of nandrolene.

Professor Tim Noakes

Tim Noakes is the Discovery Health Professor of Exercise and Sports Science at the University of Cape Town, South Africa. He is the author of Oxford's internationally acclaimed Lore of Running. He is an active sportsman in rowing, running (marathon and ultra distance) and cycling. He is also the Director of the Medical Research Council/ UCT Research Unit for Exercise Science and Sport Medicine and co-founded the Sports Science Institute of South Africa in Newlands. He is a Fellow of the American College of Sports Medicine and in 1999 he was elected as one of 22 founding members of the International Olympic Committee's Science Academy.

Professor Bengt Saltin

Bengt Saltin is Professor and Director of the Copenhagen Muscle Research Centre and is a world-renowned physiologist. Working at the August Krogh Institute, named after another famous Swedish physiologist, he has been honoured at the highest level for his contributions to physiology. These include being a member of the Royal Danish Academy of Sciences and Letters, 1984; a citation award by the American College of Sport Science in 1976; an Honor Award in 1990; and the Novo Nordisk Award in 1999. He has authored over 200 journal articles and more than 100 book chapters and reviews.

Professor Karl Wassermann

Karl Wasserman is Professor of Medicine at the cardiovascular research institute in San Francisco, California. He is best known for his work in determining anaerobic threshold in the 1970s and has continued to work in areas related to bioenergetics, cardiovascular systems, pulmonary disease and exercise. He has authored over 200 reports and publications. He is both medically trained as a doctor and a researcher in exercise physiology. It is this combination that has resulted in bringing medics and scientists together to investigate exercise physiology and pathophysiology, particularly in the case of using exercise tests to interpret data.

SUMMARY

It is impossible in such a short space to give adequate credit to the many scientists that have contributed directly or indirectly to what today we call sport and exercise science. What we can determine is that the subject had its roots in physical education and medicine. As these two areas have developed and expanded both in academia and in the applied setting, a whole new subject was created with sport and exercise as its focus.

What the next century of developments holds in store, no one is quite sure. Clearly, though, technological advances that allow researchers to observe in increasingly greater detail will again influence discoveries. Areas such as molecular biology and the Genome Project hold great potential for the understanding of our DNA and how it interacts with physical activity and exercise. In biomechanics, advances are continuing in video analysis and computerisation of movement, which can then translate precise movements into calculation of forces. In the health and exercise sciences, the study of interventions – such as the use of exercise psychology to motivate people to partake in exercise and activity, or how rehabilitative methods progress the injured patient or athlete – will continue to develop.

In all areas of work, professionals and practitioners are being challenged for evidence-based practice. This means that if a claim is made about something, then evidence must be provided to support that claim. This evidence is just a small piece in the overall research process. Often it starts with an idea and/or an observation and whether that observation or idea originates from ancient Greece, the Renaissance period or is an original thought, it will continue to be refined in the modern age.

History is replete with researchers who can be associated with what we study today, i.e., sport and exercise science. The few that have been mentioned have followed a path of enquiry that many students will follow when undertaking a project or dissertation. To acquire a sense of historical perspective allows students to demonstrate their understanding of what has occurred prior to them embarking on their own 'road of discovery'. Neither should we forget that these researchers, whether having researched in medicine, biomechanics, psychology, physics or other disciplines, have educated us. The theories that they have developed, and for which they have provided evidence, form the basis of the content for all the lectures that you attend and textbooks that you read. The continuation of this educational process, through conducting your own research project, should be viewed as a noble and time-honoured pursuit.

2

LITERATURE REVIEW

First get your facts; and then you can distort them at your leisure.
Mark Twain (1835–1910)

LEARNING OUTCOMES

Following this chapter you should be able to:

1 understand the importance of a literature review;
2 know how to prepare to write a literature review;
3 undertake the writing of a literature review; and
4 review the strengths and weaknesses of a literature review.

Introduction

In many programmes of study, students are often asked to review literature. These assignments can take many formats. A common format is a reading task whereby students are asked to read a variety of books and journals to identify a topic of interest so as to be able to detail important knowledge related to the topic. Alternatively, students often complete a laboratory report or have to write up a study in the style of a journal article. The introduction that often forms the first section of these reports is very similar to a review of the literature, only in a condensed form. This chapter will explore the processes and product of a literature review that a student might have to write for a dissertation or independent study project.

The literature review may be seen as an arduous process but it is an important part of the dissertation process. It allows the student to consider and support the research *a priori* (before the fact) to collecting data. The literature review is written to support the research question or hypotheses that a student will write prior to their collection of data. However, much of this material could equally be applied in principle to introductory sections of laboratory reports or an assignment involving a critical commentary of a topic in sport and exercise science.

Why is a literature review so important?

A literature review should not be perceived as a way of padding out a dissertation or as a way of lengthening your bibliography merely to satisfy your tutor. The more thorough the literature review, the more confident and knowledgeable you will be about your chosen topic. The literature is crucial because it demonstrates a number of key skills; if a student is able to demonstrate these key skills, they are giving themselves every opportunity to perform well on the assignment.

The first skill that is demonstrated is not necessarily a skill but more a characteristic of personality, namely attitude. Students who quickly realise the value and importance of a thorough review of literature make the connection that the time spent on the literature review will save them time at the end of the process. Students who are prepared to undertake a thorough review of literature prior to the experiment beginning can be secure in the knowledge that they are setting themselves up with the best possible strategy for success.

It becomes quickly apparent to a tutor which students have latched on to the first article they find and have failed to read around the topic. They demonstrate a limited understanding of what has been done before, who performed the studies, how long ago the studies were performed, and what are the current directions of studies. These are all important skills when reviewing the literature. A good review is not concentrated on one or two articles, as this does not provide a critical synthesis of the literature. It is important to realise that a thorough review will prevent you from performing work that is superficial and that would undermine your final conclusions.

In undergraduate work, often the demonstration of working through a formalised process is as important as the final dissertation. However, a student who is aware of repetitious experiments can always implement subtle changes to give their experiment a slightly different aim or purpose. Therefore, one of the main purposes of a literature review is to demonstrate a critical synthesis of the literature connected to the chosen topic. Using this descriptor as the main purpose, the importance of a review can be divided into two sections: first, what you (the student) do prior to writing the review (*the process*) and second, what you write (*the product*). Both are equally important because a poor process will lead to a poor product and will be reflected in a review that lacks understanding, depth of knowledge and critical commentary. Equally, conducting a thorough review (the process) but producing a review that is poorly written and organised haphazardly will not demonstrate your ability to critically synthesise and will more than likely score poorly.

The purpose of a review of literature

The main purpose of a literature review is critical synthesis and this should link to Chapter 3 by establishing your question or questions for your dissertation or project. By the end of your literature review, you should have a very clear idea of what has been conducted before, what the strengths and weaknesses of the work are, and what future projects could be conducted. In short, you should be an 'expert' in that idea, knowing more than your fellow student and probably knowing the literature as well as your lecturer (if not better). In the following sections, specific reference is made to five points and you should attempt to demonstrate how these points relate to your chosen topic. More will be discussed about how to accomplish this in the sections on how to plan, prepare and write the literature review.

Planning and preparation

To answer the question 'How do I go about the planning and preparation stages?', subdivide the review into several divisions:

1   Define and narrow the research problem.
2   Place the study in a historical context.
3   Acknowledge replication.
4   Discover recommendations of others for future projects.
5   Sample current opinion and controversies.

The first part of this process is realising that there are no short-cuts and you should appreciate that the literature review will take time. How much prior knowledge you have in your chosen topic will clearly influence where you start in relation to your review. Students selecting topics that they know little about will clearly need to do more groundwork not only on the literature but also on the fundamental theories behind the topic. Therefore, a useful strategy is to choose a topic that you are interested in and one that you have some knowledge about. Borg and Gall (1989) suggest seven steps to a literature review:

1   Define the research topic.
2   State the specific purpose of the review.
3   Select the database(s).
4   Select descriptors.
5   Plan.
6   Conduct.
7   Review.

Define the research area

Reading assignments that are often used to select a topic are not as thorough as a review of literature, but in most selected topics in sport and exercise science there are usually enough published studies that relate to your chosen topic. If there are not, then you may wish to speak to your tutor as to whether this is going to create too much work or whether the challenge of the limited studies will add a certain amount of originality to your work. Consider how you work best. If you are someone who likes a challenge and is able to conceptualise well and use other examples from other disciplines, then the lack of previous studies should not put you off. If you are a student who prefers a more clear-cut framework to develop your study, then it may be better to select a topic that has a variety of studies from which to work. Once you have selected a topic to investigate, you need to plan how to begin the literature review.

State the specific purpose of the search

The following is a hypothetical example of a student who wishes to investigate the effects of creatine on sprint performance. The student has heard his fellow students talking about taking creatine and improving their sprint performance in sports such as football, hockey and rugby. The student is then interested to find out whether this is true. In this example the student has begun to determine the focus of the question; the more precise the question in terms of the component parts, the more specific the literature review. This will then naturally lead on to other specific decisions, e.g.:

- the population to be studied, e.g. children, adults, elderly, male/female;
- the intervention used, the conditions of the experiment or the dates;
- the type of variables measured, e.g. body fat, body mass, water loss;
- the design of the studies, e.g. single case studies, random controlled studies.

Select database(s) and descriptors

The library is the key resource in searching for literature; the more you are able to use all the resources offered by the library, the more thorough your review will be. The key resources that you should use within the library for your literature review are:

1   electronic databases – searches relevant key words;
2   books – relevant information and a key resource;
3   current journal articles – offers most recent research;
4   newspapers – most up to date but limited in depth of material;
5   encyclopaedias – limited source of information;
6   dissertations/theses held in library or department – in-depth research;
7   electronic table of contents alerts, such as zetoc alert, which sends a monthly table of contents alerts from journals selected by you straight to your inbox.

One of the first places to start your search is through the electronic databases to which most libraries have access. The main database used in ESS is one called SportsDiscus. Other databases that might have some relevance to topics related to ESS are PsychLit (a database related to mainstream psychology), Web of Science (a database related to science information) and MedLine (a database related to the medical sciences). Most databases work on the same principle: by entering key words, names of authors, or dates of publications into the database, articles and books will be highlighted that relate to your topic. In our hypothetical example, our student knows from one of their physiology lectures that creatine often comes under the heading of ergogenic aids (Figure 2.1). Using key words is not as straightforward as it seems because typing in 'ergogenic aids' might highlight hundreds of studies related to ergogenic aids, including studies on many substances other than creatine. However, reading some general review articles on the use of ergogenic aids and athletic performance will allow for some breadth to the topic and also identify any common themes. Remember that one of the key purposes is to begin to narrow your review down to the specifics of your topic. One of the methods to narrow the review and search is to search by author, by title, or perhaps to combine words. If you know a particular author has published papers on creatine, then it is likely they have published previous studies on the topic. If you combine words, take care because different words, although meaning the same, often produce very different results. However, combining two specific words is a good way of reducing the number of studies.

Perhaps one of the common themes you would identify in reading around the topic of ergogenics is that the literature identifies that ergogenic aids do work but it appears that for certain people they have no effect whatsoever. Therefore, you might decide that armed with this fact, you would try to identify those for whom the creatine might be most effective (Figure 2.2). For example, participants who are already using creatine are unlikely to benefit from more creatine, whereas participants who are vegetarians and

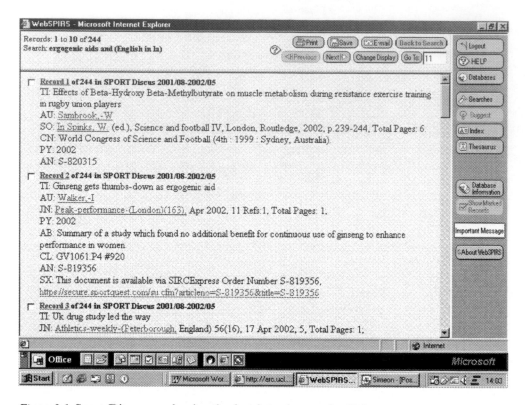

Figure 2.1 SportsDiscus search using the descriptor 'ergogenic aids'

often lower in creatine might benefit more within your study. After you begin to get an idea of the general literature about ergogenic aids, you might consider limiting your SportsDiscus search to topics specifically related to creatine studies. Entering 'creatine' as a word search will again produce hundreds of studies because there will be many different sports which have examined this problem. For example, if you are interested in studying the effects of creatine on sprint running performance, there will be journal papers that will have investigated this topic, but it might also be worthwhile reading some journal papers related to sprint cycling to see if there is any cross-over of know-ledge that could be applicable to your study. It is important to remember that databases are only as accurate as the people responsible for inputting the data, so you should consider using more than one resource.

Another useful technique is to obtain the most up-to-date article that you can find on your chosen topic. Then using the reference list from your article, you can begin to read some of the articles of interest. If the article you obtain is a review article such as ones produced in the journal *Sports Medicine*, then there will be a large number of relevant references. This will provide signposting and give you a good start for further information. When you have selected some references that include your topic of study, you should check that your library has these journals in stock. If your library does not stock these journals, it is possible to ask the library to obtain an inter-library loan for you. This is a system whereby the library will make a request, usually from the British

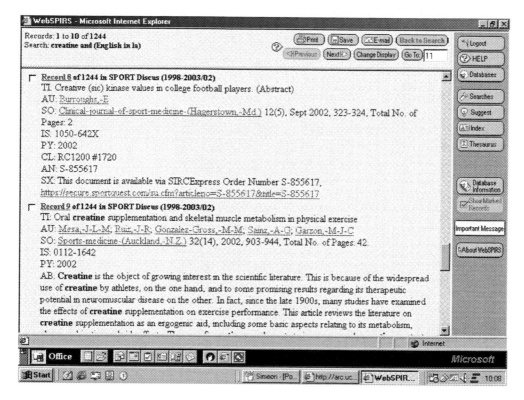

Figure 2.2 SportsDiscus search using the descriptor 'creatine'

Library, for a photocopy of the published article. There is a cost to this facility and current charges are about £5–£6 per article. Prior to requesting an inter-library loan, it is worth printing the abstract before purchasing to ensure that it is relevant and vital to your review. In some universities and colleges the department might provide for a limited number of inter-library loans per student, so it is worth enquiring if this is available to you. However, remember that in using a review article to obtain your references, it is possible that other articles that could be of use to you may have been omitted. It is only one author's perspective, therefore be aware that when reviewing other people's work, you are getting their perspective. One aspect of your project is to put together literature that demonstrates *your* perspective on the topic.

Other resources such as newspapers and encyclopaedias should also be consulted, as although they are examples of secondary source material, newspapers can provide topical up-to-date information. Encyclopaedias can also give a broad definitive perspective of the topic. Most libraries carry copies of dissertations and theses, which are based on an individual, in-depth, independent study and will give you some ideas about structure and organisation of the literature review. Take care that any information used from these sources is referenced correctly to avoid plagiarism. There are guidelines on how to present work, but just because a particular thesis or dissertation approached a certain section in a particular way, does not mean that it is the right approach for you. Discuss these matters with your tutor but also have the confidence to make your own judgements.

Therefore, in summary, the three key points in this section are to:

1 consult widely;
2 reference carefully;
3 create your own perspective.

Plan

Once you have consulted many journal articles, books etc that you have read, noted or photocopied, you may find that information overload becomes a problem. You need to decide what is important and what is peripheral. This is the time to consider all the information you have and to devise a plan for bringing it together into a coherent format. A vital technique is to keep an accurate record of all the articles that you have reviewed. Most of the electronic databases allow you to print out your literature search. Ensuring that this is filed carefully should provide an effective record. Some students use file cards, writing the authors' names, year of publication, title of publication, title of journal, volume number and page numbers. This is the minimum amount of information that you should record, but it is also useful to include some pertinent details regarding subject numbers, key results and the main conclusions.

It is just as easy to use computer software to create a database for references. Microsoft MS Access is a possibility for just such a task. Do not forget page numbers for quotes. If you are on a limited budget in terms of the amount of photocopying, then this is an economical system to use (Figure 2.3). Depending on how complex or thorough you wish to make your summary, you can add more variables and clearly these can be customised to suit your needs. If you are haphazard about recording your references, you can bet that when it comes to writing your reference list, the crucial reference you need will be the one you cannot find. Therefore, be methodological and record the information carefully and thoroughly in one central place – a folder or file is ideal.

When you begin to write the literature review, it is worth thinking of it as analogous to a funnel (Figure 2.4). At the beginning of the review, broad and generalised themes will be introduced. As you move through the review there should be a narrowing of the themes and related topics that are discussed, just like the thinner part of a funnel. At the end point of a funnel, if a tiny droplet of liquid were to drop out, this droplet would represent the critical elements of the review and lead into what are the aims and hypotheses of the study.

In summary, having identified your topic, you need to conduct the search and find information that is relevant to your area. This will involve spending a significant amount of time in the library. Try to plan ahead by thinking of descriptors prior to going onto the databases: some libraries only allow students to log on for limited amounts of time, therefore you do not want to waste time thinking about what descriptors to use. Once you have a record of the articles that you would like to read, file a record of them carefully. Another strategy is to ask the lecturers and see if they have a personal photocopy of the article. Although you will not be able to photocopy it as you would be breaking copyright regulations, if you use the summary sheets you could take away the most important points.

Author(s) ————————————————————————————

Year of publication ——————————

Title of article ————————————————————————

Journal title ——————————————————————————

Vol. and page # ————————————

Experimental design ————————————————————

Subject # ———————————————————————————

Experimental methods ————————————————————

——————————————————————————————

Key results ———————————————————————————

——————————————————————————————

Comments ——————————————————————————

——————————————————————————————

——————————————————————————————

Figure 2.3 Example of a literature review summary sheet

Conduct

Figure 2.5 is a completed literature review summary sheet that has been compiled as a result of a literature search related to oxygen kinetics. The pertinent information is recorded and summarised and will provide an aide-mémoire for the student. This also means that the student will not have to keep reading the whole journal article every time some information is needed.

How to write the review

Review

Prior to writing the review, it is good practice if a plan is produced outlining the themes to be covered. The review should begin with broad topics that have a connection with the subject matter but which will not be discussed in depth. This strategy will allow the reader to be introduced to the topic in a general way before the more complex and in-depth material is discussed. It is also worthwhile at the beginning of the review to state the purpose of the literature review so that you can place the review in context for the

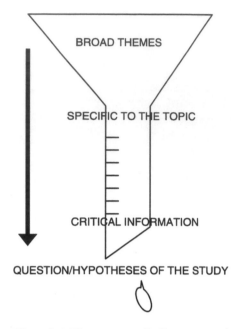

BROAD THEMES

SPECIFIC TO THE TOPIC

CRITICAL INFORMATION

QUESTION/HYPOTHESES OF THE STUDY

Figure 2.4 The concept of a literature review as a funnel

reader. It is also worthwhile to point out to the reader what the review is *not* intended to do. One strategy to implement, if you do not particularly wish to review a peripheral aspect of your topic, is to point readers to other reviews that have been published. For example, in the case of the student investigating creatine and short-term performance, a student might not wish to discuss the medical implications of taking creatine. There-fore, the reader could be directed to a relevant review article, which has discussed the health consequences of athletes taking creatine. Most reviews follow a conventional pattern; firstly a broad opening paragraph introducing the topic to the reader, followed by a statement related to the purpose of the review. The review is characterised by starting broadly and narrowing in focus, ending with the research questions or the hypotheses.

Once the writing of the review has begun, it is important to consider how the informa-tion to be included is selected. Remember, there will be a lot of information and what is not included is just as important as what is included. The most common mistake made by undergraduate students is to include too much material; *synthesis* of information is the key. It is important that you are able to demonstrate that you have an understanding of the chosen topic and are aware of any recent developments. Another important consideration is stating how the selected information links to the objectives of your study. Through adhering to these points, you will be able to safeguard against inclusion of information that is superfluous.

During the writing of the review, a decision will have to be made about how to organise and order the information in a logical manner. One common mistake to avoid is writing the review in a chronological or author order. Reviews written in this manner often end up being stilted and boring. It is more effective if the review is organised by clustering the information according to topics or ideas. By adopting this strategy, it can

---

Author(s)   Williams, C.A., Carter, H., Jones, A.M. and Doust, J.H.

Year of Publication   2001

Title of article   Oxygen uptake kinetics during treadmill running in boys and men

Journal Title Journal of Applied Physiology

Vol. and Page #   90, 1700-1706

Experimental design Comparative study between 11-12 year old boys and men aged between 21-36

Subject #   Eight boys and eight men

Experimental methods 6 minutes running exercise at 2 different running speeds corresponding to 80% of $\dot{V}O_2$ at lactate threshold and 50% of the difference between $\dot{V}O_2$ at lactate threshold and $\dot{V}O_2$ max.

Key results   No significant difference (NSD) at moderate exercise for the time constant for the primary response. Gain of the primary significantly greater in boys than men (239.1 ±7.5 vs 167.7 ±5.4 ml·kg^{-1}·km^{-1}). For heavy exercise $\dot{V}O_2$ on-kinetics were significantly faster in boys than men (14.9 ±1.1 vs 19 ±1.6 s).

Comments $\dot{V}O_2$ responses at the onset of moderate and heavy exercise are different between boys and men, there is a tendency for boys to have a faster on-kinetics and a greater initial increase in $\dot{V}O_2$ for a given increase in running speed.

Figure 2.5 Example of a completed literature review summary sheet

be demonstrated that you can also think conceptually and link themes together in an order other than chronologically.

Another common mistake is that although students compare and contrast studies, they often neglect to state how the study has contributed or failed to increase the knowledge related to the topic. Do not be afraid to be critical and judge these studies by stating how valid, trustworthy or problematic the studies and their results are. Also ensure that the methods and designs are evaluated. Often students get so preoccupied in comparing and evaluating the results of studies that they can forget to comment critically on whether the design of the experiment was appropriate. As you will have probably had at least one research methods or statistics module, you should be able to evaluate critically the experiment and the results. If you have not had an opportunity to take these modules, then reading this chapter in conjunction with Chapter 9 will help.

Thomas and Nelson (1990) pose three questions related to the critical evaluation of a literature review:

1   Is the plan developed within a reasonable theoretical framework?
2   Is current and relevant research cited and properly interpreted?
3   Is the statement of the problem clear, concise, testable and derived from the theory and research revised?

If the answer is 'yes' to all three questions, then you can be confident of having performed a thorough job. However, if the answer is 'no' or if you are uncertain, then you should go through the questions and try to ascertain the reasons for your uncertainty.

Is the plan developed within a reasonable theoretical framework?

If the answer is 'no' to this question, you should examine the theoretical concepts and check to see whether the concepts have been adequately described and critically discussed. Also check to see whether the discussion has related the theory to the applied practice. For example, has the theory related to creatine supplementation been discussed in the context of its use in endurance events, when the theoretical mechanism suggests that it can only work in short-term, high-energy power events?

Is current and relevant research cited and properly interpreted?

If the answer is 'no', then check research articles within the last two years: are all the referenced articles from 10 years ago? If so, is this because no one has done any further research? (Perhaps this is telling you that most researchers feel the major findings have been found and confirmed.) The dates of the reference list is one of the easiest ways to see how current the review is, so ensure that it is as up to date as possible. However, take care not just to cite papers that are current and up to date but which can only be found in obscure journals. Lecturers will know that it has not been possible to read this article and you are therefore just citing it as an additional source of reference, so balance the review and cite accurately.

Is the statement of the problem clear, concise, testable and derived from the theory and research revised?

If the answer is 'no' to this third question, then ask yourself the following: If someone read the literature review, would they be able to guess what my question or hypothesis is for the study? Is it obvious from the information reviewed what I am interested in studying? Successful students in the past have got one of their peers, who might know some of the literature connected to the topic, to read through the review and give feedback. Then the review is passed to someone who does not know anything about the topic. If the second person can understand the aim of the study through the review, then you have probably achieved your objective.

Finally, ensure that your review has a summary in which you draw together all the key findings connected to the topic and explicitly state where you think there are gaps in the knowledge. Table 2.1 is an example of a student's summary table related to the effects of exercise on feelings in relation to an exercise psychology dissertation. Also remember not just to summarise the key findings but also to summarise any deficiencies in the methodologies (e.g., not enough studies conducted with female participants; too few related to running etc.). Lastly, do not forget to provide the rationale for the research question or hypotheses.

Table 2.1 A summary review table extracted from a student dissertation

Study	Participants	Design and treatment	EFI results and conclusions
Gauvin & Rejeski (1993)	3 conditions selected: 1. 40 university females from University in southeast USA 2. 40 subjects randomly selected from an initial sample of 154 (88% female) attending University in eastern Canada 3. 40 subjects selected from sample of 246 (50% female) attending University in southeast USA	20 participants Ex for 25 mins, 20 participants Ex for 40 mins. Ex was with no social interaction in Lab. Completed EFI pre–during–post Ex. Ex. Classes of: impact aerobics, aerobic dance. Completed post Ex EFI. Pre Ex EFI measurement only in classrooms of 20–35 students.	S_{ig} differences for all 4 subscales ($P < 0.0001$). PEN was higher ($P < 0.0001$) post Ex class than lab setting pre or post Ex Lab PEN not S_{ig} different. REV higher in classroom pre Ex than both lab pre or post Ex. Greater REV ($P < 0.003$) after Ex in lab than classroom pre Ex. PEX not S_{ig} different post both experiences. Ex class had lower PEX pre exercise than classroom. TRA S_{ig} higher in lab Ex condition ($P < 0.002$) than in classroom prior to exercise. No S_{ig} difference between Ex groups or between real world Ex and TRA reported in classroom prior to EX. Evidence provided that the EFI is useful for Ex situations, and provides good interaction with social dimension of physical activity. Data show satisfactory psychometric properties for various physical activities.
Bozoain, Rejeski & McAuley (1994)	36 female undergraduate students. Classified into low or high self-efficacy scores.	Testing on Monark cycle ergometers. 7 mins warm up, 20 mins at 70% maximum age related heart rate reserve. EFI administered pre, 15 mins starting (during) and 10 mins post Ex.	S_{ig} multivariate interaction ($P < 0.01$), PEN ($P < 0.01$) and REV ($P < 0.01$) responsible for this. High self-efficacy group increased PEN pre-to-post Ex ($P < 0.05$). Low self-efficacy decreased PEN pre-to-post Ex ($P < 0.05$). For all subjects TRA increased after Ex ($P < 0.01$), and PEX decreased after Ex ($P < 0.01$). More efficacious females experienced greater positive feeling states during and following Ex, specifically maintaining a sense of energy and REV. paper supports reliability and validity of EFI.

Table 2.1 continued

Study	Participants	Design and treatment	EFI results and conclusions
Rejeski, Hobson, Norris & Gauvin (1995)	80 moderately fit women recruited from health and fitness.	Participants assigned to 1 of 4 protocols: 1. 10 mins attention control 2. 10 mins of Ex 3. 25 mins of Ex 4. 40 mins of Ex Ex was set at an intensity of 70% age-related heart rate reserve, on Monark cycle ergometers.	Pre-test scores not significantly different. S_{ig} time main effect ($P < 0.0001$), was superseded by S_{ig} treatment*time interaction term ($P < 0.01$). S_{ig} time effects for PEN ($P < 0.03$), TRA ($P < 0.0001$) and REV ($P < 0.0001$). REV had S_{ig} treatment*time effect ($P < 0.0008$). Data from study support position that mental health consequences of Ex in women are mediated, in part by Fs that occur during activity itself. Potential limitations derived from dose response relationship as used in field of exercise physiology, when related to the impact of various biomedical diseases.
Gauvin, Rejeski & Norris (1996)	108 women (96 from local YMCA fitness classes; 12 employees at university in north America. 83 provided data.	EFI completed 4 times a day (at random intervals between 0800 and 2200) for a total of 6 weeks as well as pre and post EX, that lasted longer than 20 minutes.	86 women reported 709 bouts of Ex. Involvement in physical activity was associated with S_{ig} increases in PEN ($P < 0.001$), REV ($P < 0.0001$) and TRA ($P < 0.0001$). No S_{ig} effects for PEX. Acute physical activity is related to S_{ig} improvements in a naturalistic setting. Pre activity scores influences pre-post change, especially if they were feeling worse. Physical activity is correlational with response, do not imply cause effect relationship.
Vlachopoulos, Biddle & Fox (1996)	304 school students, from one comprehensive and one private school in the southwest England.	Children performed in groups of 15–20 in a performance orientated 800-metre race, after the run they completed an EFI.	Psychometric properties of the EFI for children were examined. There was good fit to the data using confirmatory factor analysis on the four-factor oblique model.
Gauvin, Rejeski, Norris & Lutes (1997)	72 sedentary men and women, participants contact by telephone. Individuals were selected if they reported less than one bout of physical activity in the last month. Those who participated were remunerated $75 for their participation.	Equal numbers of male and females were randomly assigned to aerobic Ex at 3 intensities: 30%, 50% and 70% age-related heart rate reserve. Each participant went to an attention control session as the control condition. EFI's completed pre and post control/exercise.	The dependent variables were not influenced by; participants' gender, gender of the experimenter or of the control or Ex condition. PEX was the only subscale which showed there was influence of exercise intensity. Results indicated that there was no evidence for extensive mood-enhancing effects or a dose-response relationship.

Table 2.1 continued

Study	Participants	Design and treatment	EFI results and conclusions
Szabo, Mesko, Caputo & Gill (1998)	195 individuals, who were considered habitual exercisers, primarily from college communities.	Four groups were split into aerobic dance, weight-training, martial arts, tai-chi and yoga, and music appreciation (control) each group completed EFI's on three occasions, 5 mins. before and after Ex and 3 hours after Ex.	The internal consistency for the four subscales ranged from 0.77 to 0.91. Results provide evidence that low physical exertion activity can have affective beneficence that is comparable to, and some aspects greater than higher intensity aerobic or anaerobic activity. Greater TRA was reported by tai-chi and hatha yoga group (low physical exertion).

Reproduced courtesy of Mr. Andrew Soundy.

Below is a list of typical problems faced by students when presented with the challenge of writing a literature review. Below each question is some practical advice about how to resolve the problem and move on to the next stage in writing.

Common problems

1   Too much material

Solution: Examine your information to see if some studies are concluding the same things. If so, lump all the studies together and paraphrase, stating that studies w, x, y and z all found such and such. Consider using summary tables.

2   Where do I start?

Solution: Consider by reflecting on what you are interested in, and review articles that are close to your topic of interest. Have any of the studies identified problems or controversies? Can you construct a problem or question to address? If you are still unsure, go back to the seven-point plan (see p. 14).

3   How do I know when to finish?

Solution: This is always a difficult one for some students, as the deadline date and how organised the student has been will ultimately decide it. However, if you have followed a plan and worked methodologically, time should not be a problem. But do not imagine that by delaying the finish of the work it will somehow enhance the review. Often students just end up adding more and more information, which displaces the plan and makes the work look disjointed. If you stick to your plan, have the confidence to say that you have finished and you are not going to do any more work on it. Overall, you are going to be guided by the timelines and deadline dates set for you by your department.

4   How do I link themes?

Solution: Check to see how the themes are linked, use headings and subheadings to create a map or contents list of your review. Do any look out of place? If so, play around with moving some of the text from one section to another. This is one great advantage of working on the computer, in that you can easily cut and paste sections. Check to see if the themes start broad and end narrow.

5   **How many words should it be?**
Solution: This will be dependent on two factors. First, any word count stipulated by your department. Stick to this rule and show that you are able to delimit and synthesise the information accordingly. Second, it is dependent on the topic you choose and how much access to literature you have had available in order to produce the work. Overall, do not get too preoccupied with the number of words, more important is the quality of writing such as its conciseness, precision, currency and the level of criticism.

6   **How do I use quotes?**
Solution: Students often make the mistakes of having quotes on every page, possibly to demonstrate that they have read a wide variety of papers. However, this soon becomes boring and tedious. Use quotes sparingly and only where you think they will make a major impact, typically at the beginning of the review to set the scene. Take care to reference the quotes accurately.

Below is a list of common mistakes students typically make in producing their review of literature. Ensuring that adequate time has been spent on preparation for the review can prevent most of these. In their enthusiasm to collect their data, students often spend too little time in preparing and planning and hence there are gaps in their knowledge. There is also the feeling that once the data are collected, the student can go back to the literature and fill in the gaps that he or she did not have time to cover prior to the data collection. In many cases students realise that the data they have collected cannot answer the question they had set themselves. Hence they then have to spend the time re-jigging the study to fit the data. A more thorough literature review would have prevented this problem. Tables 2.2 and 2.3 should help you to prepare and evaluate your literature review.

Common mistakes

- Focus too broad or too narrow. When the focus is too broad, there is no depth to the subject matter. When it is too narrow, often numerous studies related to topic have been omitted.
- Failure to limit the topic, thereby including peripheral elements in the dissertation or report which merely confuse the reader.
- Concentrates too much on findings, overlooking important information on methodology etc.
- Over-reliance on secondary sources. Although this will be problematic if your access to resources is limited, you should always try to get to the primary sources to ensure accuracy.

Table 2.2 What is the difference between a good literature review and a poor one?

Good literature review	Poor literature review
• Purpose of the review stated.	• Lacks a stated purpose.
• Well-defined boundaries to the review, including why some material included and others omitted.	• No real boundaries to the review, some material appears irrelevant to the topic and trivial.
• Majority of references are primary sources with selective use of secondary sources.	• Majority of references are secondary sources, limited use of primary sources leading to a descriptive superficial review.
• Recent controversies and/or methodological developments discussed in review.	• No comments regarding controversial issues or methodological developments. Often an over-reliance on just reviewing the results from studies.
• Selected literature is pertinent to the problem.	• Too much literature is not directly related to the problem
• Bibliographic references are complete.	• Bibliographic references are missing or incomplete.
• There are numerous examples of criticism of the design and methodology of important studies.	• Study methodologies are simply reported as if they possess no weaknesses.
• Studies are compared and contrasted, comment is made regarding conflicting or inconclusive results.	• Mostly descriptive of what each study found without the student forming an opinion about the relative merits of the studies.
• The student is able to make it clear to the reader how the references apply to the problem.	• Interpretation of the relevance of the studies often left to the reader's discretion.
• Effective summary of the overall interpretation and understanding of current knowledge. Often uses summary tables to good effect.	• There is no conclusion or summary paragraph. Literature review just peters out.
• The reader is able to identify the theoretical rationale for the research question or hypotheses.	• The reader is left confused or unsure as to what exactly will be the research question or hypotheses.

Table 2.3 Checklist for a literature review

Contents	Yes	No
Have you stated the purpose of the review?		
Have you limited the scope of the review?		
Have you cited a range of years?		
Have you cited predominantly primary sources as opposed to secondary sources?		
Have you stated any recent developments related to your topic?		
Is your literature relevant to the topic?		

Table 2.3 continued

Contents	Yes	No
Are all your references complete?		
Have you organised your review by topics and ideas rather than by author or time line?		
Have you begun the review with information broadly related to the topic and ending with information most closely related to it?		
Have major studies been discussed in detail and minor ones all grouped together?		
Have you criticised the design and methodology of studies?		
Have you compared and contrasted studies and noted inconclusive studies?		
Have you provided a summary?		
Does the summary provide for a current understanding of the topic?		
Can the reader understand based on the theory, why you are justified in proposing your hypotheses or question?		
Can the reader understand why you have chosen the methodology or design that you are proposing to use in your study?		

SUMMARY

- Devote time to search for as much literature connected to your topic as is possible.
- Keep adequate notes of where you found the literature and, if necessary, begin a reference list or summary sheet.
- Before writing the review, outline a plan using headings and subheadings to guide you as to where to include information.
- Begin writing the review with the information that is *least* connected to the problem and end with the information that is *most closely* connected to the problem.
- Adhere to word counts as laid down by the department.
- Use summary tables to synthesise large amounts of information, which perhaps all show the same results or conclusions.
- Be willing to highlight controversies and be prepared to give some opinions about why this is the case.
- Remember, the key objective of the review is to synthesise a large amount of literature in a critical and informative manner so that a reader will be able to understand the relevant issues related to the topic.

3

EXPERIMENTAL DESIGN

No single experiment can establish the absolute proof of the falsity of
the null hypothesis no matter how improbable the outcome of the
experiment under the null hypothesis.

Allen Edwards (1968)

LEARNING OUTCOMES

Following this chapter you should be able to:

1   outline issues relating to validity;
2   explain reliability and associated terms;
3   identify different types of experimental design;
4   select the appropriate experimental design for your research project.

Introduction

Experimental design refers to the way in which an experiment is structured. It is rarely
something that is made explicit to the novice researcher and consequently is often
overlooked in the planning stage. By the time you have identified your research question
(Chapter 2) and translated this into your research hypotheses (Chapter 1), you should
begin considering how you are going to design your research project. This chapter will
introduce issues such as validity and reliability and focus on some common research
designs, with the aim of giving you the understanding required to design an experiment
that is appropriate to your research question.

Common mistakes

The two major mistakes that undergraduate students make are:

1   complicating research projects because they are unclear about the research
    question;
2   deciding on the wrong type of research design to answer their research question.

The research question and experimental design

Before addressing the details of experimental design, remember:

1   The research question is absolutely central to the entire project; it should reflect the
    experimental design.

2   The formulated question will determine the type of design you employ, the type of statistics you use, and the depth of discussion and conclusion relating to your initial question.
3   The research question you have constructed may prove to be too difficult to answer; this problem cannot be solved through clever experimental design.
4   Above all, it is the research question that should be leading the experimental design, not vice versa.

Validity

Validity is commonly used to indicate the soundness of an argument, as in 'she's got a valid point'. However, within the context of scientific study, it has a very specific meaning. Although there are many types of validity, a general definition may be: 'the surety that we are measuring what we think we are measuring'.

Internal validity

Internal validity relates to the conditions and design of the actual study. It tells us how certain we are that the results of the experiment are due to the independent variable(s) that we were monitoring. For instance, an experiment examining the effects of smoking cessation on aerobic fitness would have high internal validity if it could be demonstrated that any changes in aerobic fitness were as a result of the subjects' stopping smoking. The internal validity would be low if it was uncertain whether these changes occurred because of smoking cessation or another factor that was not accounted for, such as an increase in the amount of training.

Threats to internal validity

Numerous factors can impinge upon the internal validity of an experiment. It is essential that a scientist, at the very least, acknowledge these influences and should ideally minimise their impact through a sound experimental design.

In the sport and exercise science field, common threats to internal validity include:

- measurement techniques;
- subject history;
- subject selection;
- subject mortality;
- regression to the mean.

Measurement techniques

The instrumentation or tests used to measure subjects can weaken internal validity in many ways. A technique that is unreliable will give inconsistent results for subjects who actually possess the same value for a variable (e.g. body mass). It then becomes difficult to attribute changes in this variable to a treatment that may have been used (e.g. dieting), as these changes may be due to the unreliable equipment alone. Thus, the reliability (see p. 34) of a technique should always be assessed in advance of its use in a study. Another important consideration is the accuracy of a technique. A set of scales may be very reliable, producing very consistent scores for an individual, but they may consistently be reading 5 kg too high. The accuracy of an untested measurement method can be analysed by assessing the criterion validity (see p. 34) of the technique.

Subject history

Without having a detailed appreciation of a subject's history, the internal validity of the study will suffer. There are many factors in an individual's history that may influence their scores on a given variable. A runner may show a rapid response to a new training regime, not because of the effectiveness of the training regime, but because they were previously injured and have recently begun their return to full training. Without understanding the history of subjects, the reason behind a finding can be easily misinterpreted. It is also necessary to know the details of the testing history of subjects. Have they performed any tests prior to their participation in your study? Subjects who have conducted tests many times may be further into the learning effect (see p. 35) than less experienced subjects.

Subject selection

The way in which subjects are selected for an experiment can have profound effects upon the internal validity of that experiment. As scientists, we are often concerned with particular populations. These may be general populations, such as Northwest Europeans, or more specific populations, such as adult female soccer players. It is usually impossible to measure the entire population we seek to examine, so instead a sample of this population is selected to represent the population. Certain selection techniques may affect how representative this sample is. For example, a study examining the body shape of British adults may take place using the latest scanning techniques in order to give accurate and detailed measurements of each individual's dimensions. If the study asked for volunteers, would you take part? How representative of the British population is the sample likely to be? How likely are those with socially perceived undesirable body shapes to volunteer for this study? To remove the chance of the selection method influencing the characteristics of the sample, random selection of subjects is advised. This is usually very difficult to achieve in a practical situation (particularly in undergraduate research), but the possible influence of non-random selection should always be acknowledged.

Subject mortality

This term does not refer to the death of subjects, but covers the variety of reasons that lead subjects to withdraw from a study. It is entirely unethical to coerce subjects to remain within a study, so an experimenter can do little to reverse subject mortality once it has occurred. Thorough briefing regarding the demands of a study prior to the subjects' agreement to participate, together with an empathetic design of any treatment programme, may reduce the incidence of mortality. Despite any preventive measures taken by the experimenter, mortality can still occur. This becomes a major threat to internal validity when its distribution is uneven between the control and the treatment group, as more subjects drop out of one group as opposed to another group. The two groups then become incomparable. If more subjects drop out of the treatment group, then this group becomes representative only of those who can tolerate the treatment, whereas the control group still represents the original population. Any differences between the two groups at this point may stem from the difference in their constituency. This can be accounted for, to some degree, by withdrawing from the control group similar subjects to those who have withdrawn from the treatment group.

Regression to the mean

This is a phenomenon that was first rationalised by Sir Francis Galton in 1885. He found, in his study of the heredity of height, that extremely tall parents tended to have children who were tall, but were slightly shorter than their parents. The reverse was found to happen at the other end of the spectrum, where extremely short parents usually had children slightly taller than themselves. Of course, a very tall parent can have a child that is taller than they are, but the probability is higher that the child will be less tall. This is a statistical effect that shows the tendency of extreme scores to 'regress' to the mean. It applies to almost any characteristic that can be measured. Johan Cruyff is the only footballer to win the European Footballer of the Year award three times; his son Jordi, while a professional footballer, has never achieved such a distinction. Indeed, the Cruyffs are a rarity in that they have produced two generations of international footballers. How many sports stars sire a child of the same level of ability?

Regression to the mean does not just apply to the scores between generations of the same family, it also occurs with repeated scores from the same individuals. Think of using 50-metre sprint time to assess a squad's speed. Is the athlete who achieved the fastest speed on the first test going to be the fastest on the second test? Will the athlete with the slowest time for the first test be the slowest the second time around? It is possible, but if there is a difference in their performance, in which direction is it most likely to be?

Regression to the mean can often be overlooked in terms of the effect upon internal validity. Many studies divide subjects into groups based upon their score on some measure. A study may wish to examine the effect of a relaxation strategy on state anxiety prior to competition. The experimenter may divide the groups according to their scores on a state anxiety questionnaire conducted prior to competition. The experimenter could then re-test prior to another competition, when the relaxation technique has been used. The results might show that the high-state anxiety group show a reduction in state anxiety, but the low-state anxiety group show an increase in state anxiety. They could conclude that the technique is beneficial to the high-state anxiety group, but detrimental to the low-state anxiety group. This could equally be an artefact of regression to the mean, and in fact the effect of the technique may be neutral. The effect of regression to the mean can be taken into account through the use of matched control groups. These control groups are matched to be at the same end of the spectrum as the experimental groups. Theoretically, the control groups should regress to the mean in the same way as do the experimental groups. The difference in the extent of the change for the experimental and control groups can be attributed to the treatment, as opposed to the regression effect. The experimenter should always be aware of the influence of regression to the mean when interpreting any findings.

External validity

External validity is concerned with the extent to which the results of an experiment are applicable to non-experimental situations. Often, in the sport and exercise science setting, the question is how relevant are these findings to the 'real world'? The external validity is low if the results can be applied only to a particular set of circumstances. For example, a study that examines the effect of mental relaxation strategies on success in a 3-foot putting task for male golfers with a handicap of between 4 and 2 is likely to possess low external validity. External validity is high when the results can be applied to a wide range of tasks, conditions and populations.

There can be a conflict between internal and external validity. In order to ensure the results are attributable to a certain independent variable (possessing high internal validity), the conditions may have to be controlled quite tightly. This may in turn lead to the creation of an artificial set of conditions which do not reflect the real world (possessing low external validity). Similarly, in conducting an experiment that is applicable to a wide range of conditions and populations, the control of the experiment may be reduced along with the internal validity. There are no definitive rules on the balance to be struck between these two forms of validity. The issue is always specific to the purpose of the experiment and it is almost certainly a subject that you should discuss with your dissertation supervisor.

Validity of measurement

It is often desirable for a researcher to establish the validity of the measurement techniques that are employed in a given study. Specific experiments may be conducted prior to the main experiment which are designed purely to assess the validity of the measurement tools that are to be used in the main experiment. There are numerous strands of validity. Of those that are discussed here, both criterion and construct validity may be tested through an experimental model, whereas logical and ecological validity are more commonly defended through discourse.

Logical validity

Logical validity, often referred to as face validity, reflects the extent to which a logical line of reasoning exists, supporting the notion that a measurement technique does indeed measure that which it is supposed to measure. Hydrostatic weighing was initially introduced as a technique that could be logically supposed to determine body density (based upon Archimedes' principle) and ultimately, through the application of Siri's equation, used to estimate body fat percentage. It was not until this technique was compared with cadaver studies or more modern scanning techniques that these logical assumptions could begin to be verified. A measurement tool that only has logical validity should be regarded with some caution. An assumption, no matter how seemingly flawless, is still an assumption.

Criterion validity

Criterion validity is established through comparing a new or untested measurement tool against an accepted measurement technique, often called a 'gold standard'. There should be an existing body of scientific evidence that supports the accuracy and validity of the gold standard method. In this way it is reasonable to assume that if the new measure concurs with the gold standard measure, the new measure by association must be a valid technique. This type of validity is called criterion validity because it is compared to a criterion measure (i.e. the gold standard). With a new technique for measuring body composition, an experiment may seek to establish criterion validity by measuring a set of subjects using the new technique, then measure the same subjects using underwater weighing (the gold standard). Should the subjects obtain very similar results with both techniques, then it can be said that criterion validity has been established.

Construct validity

Construct validity relates to the ability of a measurement technique to detect differences between populations who are known to differ in a given 'construct'. The construct refers to the concept that is being measured. In most instances in sport and exercise science these constructs are concrete (e.g. body fat percentage, force generated, knee angle). However, in some situations the construct is more abstract and adheres more closely to the definition of this term as used in the social sciences (e.g. repeated sprint ability, training status, strength endurance). In psychology much theoretical work is required before a construct, such as anxiety or motivation, can be established. A technique for body fat measurement that did not detect differences between an anorexic population and an obese population would have poor construct validity, as it would be insensitive to the differences in the construct that are known to exist between these two groups.

Ecological validity

Ecological validity is closely related to the concept of 'specificity'. It indicates how closely the conditions under which the measurements are taken reflect the actual conditions of the real sporting or exercise environment. A test designed to predict triathletes' swimming endurance would have little ecological validity if performed in a laboratory on a cycle ergometer. To a lesser extent, if the competition were to take place in open water, the ecological validity of the test would be reduced if the test were to be performed in a 25-metre pool. Strong ecological validity is one factor that contributes to high external validity. There is sometimes a strain between designing a test that reflects the 'real' environment and a test that is controllable and contains high internal validity.

Reliability

'Reliability' as a general term refers to the consistency of a measurement technique (although a more specific definition will be introduced later in the chapter). It tells us how variable a measurement technique is, assuming that the variable being measured remains constant. The reliability of a set of scales could be assessed by measuring a constant mass on several occasions. The results for a set of scales with high reliability would be very similar each time (possessing low variability). The results for a set of scales with low reliability would differ considerably each time the constant mass was weighed (possessing high variability).

It is essential for an experimenter to have some idea of the reliability of the technique they are using and possibly to reject techniques that possess low reliability. If we were using an unreliable set of scales to measure the impact of an exercise regime on body mass, we would be unsure whether any changes were a result of the exercise regime or merely due to the variability of the scales. Reliability affects our surety in the findings of an experiment and thus impacts upon the validity of an experiment.

Sources of variability

The variability of the measurement technique, which affects the reliability, can consist of many elements. These include:

- technician error;
- equipment error;
- learning effect;
- biological variance.

We look at each of these below.

Technician error

Here, the term 'error' does not necessarily mean that something is being done incorrectly; rather it refers to the variability in the technique of the person operating the instrument or making the measurement. For example, an individual using skin-fold callipers will not always obtain the same measurement for a skin fold from the same anatomical site, from the same subject, in exactly the same condition. Technician error is usually reduced as the technician gains more experience of the technique.

Equipment error

This is variability that is inherent within the equipment used. A blood analyser may produce different results for blood lactate concentration, when two identical samples are analysed. Equipment error is usually minimised by the use of regular calibration procedures, where the equipment may be tested against a known constant and any discrepancy rectified.

Learning effect

When dealing with measures or tests of human performance, there is almost always a learning effect. There may be a technique or a strategy that a subject will improve upon each time they perform the test that is unrelated to the construct being tested. For instance, it is possible for a subject to improve their performance in the 12-minute run that is used to predict aerobic fitness, through learning to run at an optimal pace throughout the 12 minutes. Their aerobic fitness may be the same on different testing occasions, but this learning effect may lead to an increase in performance. The learning effect can usually be lessened through a familiarisation process, where the subject practises a procedure prior to the actual testing.

Biological variance

Many parameters measured in humans fluctuate on account of the inconstancy of the numerous biological processes occurring within the human body. An individual's mass may alter throughout the course of a day as a result of changes in hydration status, consumption of food, and excretion. The fact that someone is heavier when measured after lunch does not necessarily indicate a long-term trend of increasing mass. It is merely an indication that they have undergone a fluctuation within the ranges represented by biological variance. In an attempt to minimise the effects of biological variance, experimenters may try to control certain conditions relating to the subjects, such as controlling the diet and water intake of a subject or testing at the same time of day on each occasion.

It is common practice to employ a pilot study that attempts to reduce the variance arising from the four factors just discussed by making modifications to the methods and procedures. In addition to trying to improve the reliability of their measurement procedures, a pilot study can also be used to record the reliability of the measurement techniques. Undergraduate students are strongly encouraged to carry out pilot work, as although it may seem more time-consuming, the benefits are worth the extra effort.

Terminology

To investigate the various components contributing to variability, researchers have devised a series of concepts that relate to different aspects of reliability (Kadaba *et al.* 1985).

Reproducibility

Reproducibility examines the variability of measurements taken on testing occasions (usually referred to as trials) that are consecutive and have negligible time between them. EMG recordings taken from three forehand drives performed by a tennis player in a row would enable the experimenter to investigate the reproducibility of the measurement technique. In taking the measurements in close temporal proximity to one another, reproducibility attempts to look at the variability of the measurements, minus the influences of biological variance and much of the technician error stemming from setting up the equipment (e.g. placement of EMG electrodes).

Reliability

Reliability is taken as the variability that exists in measurements taken on the same day that have a time interval between them. The EMG recordings from three forehand drives performed 20 minutes apart would examine the reliability of the measurement technique. It is sometimes necessary to leave a period for a subject to rest in between trials, so that fatigue does not add to the variability.

Constancy

Constancy refers to the variability arising in measurements taken on separate days. EMG measurements taken from three different training sessions throughout a week would evaluate the constancy of the measurement technique. Constancy is usually taken to represent all the factors that contribute to the variability of a measurement tool.

Types of experimental design

There is no such thing as the perfect experimental design. Every design has strengths and weaknesses. The following section highlights some of the more commonly used structures; however, these are not mutually exclusive. It is possible that your eventual experimental model will incorporate components from more than one of the designs discussed here. The descriptions are designed to help you plan your own research and then explicitly understand and articulate what it is that you are doing. Examples and diagrams are used to facilitate your understanding of the structure of each type of experimental design.

Single subject study

As the term implies, a single subject design is defined by the fact that the sample is confined to one subject or sometimes one group. Much of the early work in education was based on single subjects or what were known as 'case studies'. Sport and exercise science psychology and sociology often use single subject study or case study designs. However, single subject experiments should not be thought of as being similar to case studies. The two are very different not only in the way they attempt to control the variance in an experiment but also in the data analyses. It is also important to recognise that these designs are neither inferior nor superior to the other designs discussed later in this chapter.

Although physiologists do not tend to use a single case subject design, in certain circumstances such as working with an elite athlete, this type of design is appropriate. The experimental control of single subject design is just as rigorous, and data collection can often be just as time-consuming, as designs that employ a control and an experimental group (see 'True experimental' and 'Quasi-experimental' designs on pp. 40–2). For a physiologist interested in knowing the effects of a relaxation technique on heart rate during a complex motor task, the first task is to record a series of baseline heart rates with the athlete performing the complex motor task. These are known as baseline measures because they identify the athlete's habitual response without any intervention. The number of baseline measures would depend on the stability of the measures and whether the researcher was convinced they had a representative picture of the heart rate during the motor task.

After the baseline measures have been collected, the second phase would be to introduce the intervention (the relaxation technique) and monitor the heart rate whilst performing the task. The researcher might have hypothesised that the heart rate will decrease and the task improve. After this phase the athlete would be asked not to follow the relaxation technique and another baseline period would be recorded. A final phase would be the re-introduction of the relaxation technique. Typically, single subject data are graphed and the responses to the consecutive stages listed below can be seen in a series of line graphs (Figure 3.1).

Stages of measurement for a single subject design:

1 Baseline
2 Intervention
3 Withdrawal of the intervention
4 Reintroduction of the intervention

Figure 3.1 shows how these stages interrelate. The success or failure of the experiment will be a reflection of the downward or upward trends of the line graphs.

Single subject experiments must be designed so that there is a high reliability of measurement techniques and thus internal validity is unaffected. This can be achieved by ensuring careful monitoring of all measurements, having systematic checks during monitoring and ensuring that factors resulting in unreliable observations are controlled. As there will be a number of repeated measurements, it is important to ensure that standardisation of protocols and procedures is followed. In physiology this does not pose too much difficulty, as most test procedures have very clear instructions. Similarly the environment within a laboratory is often held constant in terms of temperature and humidity. The introduction of the baseline and the intervention require very clear instructions about how they are to be introduced. If they are not introduced in the same way every time, there will be error within the measurements. It is important to note that the more times you introduce and withdraw the intervention, the more likely the chance of error.

One of the reasons for obtaining baseline measures is to ascertain the variation in the measure. In most situations, by measuring the same variable twice it is unlikely that an identical result will be achieved; if it were then we would very easily be able to measure the intervention effect. However, most measurements recorded more than once vary and it is this variation that is so important to the experiment. If the variation is so large, then it is possible that any intervention effect will not be big enough to show a difference. In this example you either need to use a different measure, that is more sensitive and precise, or you will have to create a standard for determining when the baseline is stable (e.g. no more than a 2 per cent variation on the mean heart rate over

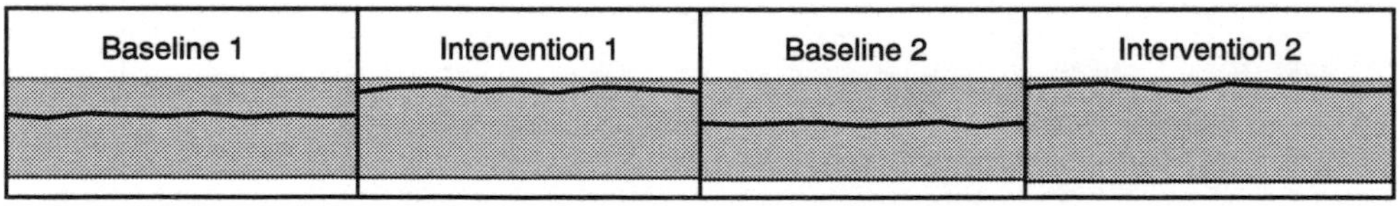

Baseline 1	Intervention 1	Baseline 2	Intervention 2

Figure 3.1 Single subject design

the last 15 seconds of each minute). As a general rule of thumb, there should be the same number of measurements in the baseline and the intervention and both should be of the same time duration. It is preferable if the experiment ends with the intervention phase rather than ending negatively with the baseline.

The major weakness of the single subject design is the low external validity. The results from the subject are often difficult to generalise to the wider population. Although a weakness, researchers should not be put off by this approach; for instance when working with Olympic athletes it is unlikely that you would wish to generalise the results to a wider audience. It is also highly unlikely that you would be able to gather a large enough group of Olympic athletes to form an experimental and control group. The way to improve on the low external validity is to perform replication studies whereby the single subject design is conducted several times using exactly the same protocols and with similar subjects.

Longitudinal design

Longitudinal studies are ones in which the aim of the study is to collect data at different points in time so that changes can be observed in the measured variables. Longitudinal studies are a particular feature in paediatric research, because they allow the researcher to follow changes in growth and maturation and to chart how these two factors affect performance in such variables as aerobic and anaerobic power, strength, and speed etc. The design is very strong because it does not rely on a single time point from which to gain an insight into the measured variables. However, there are a number of disadvantages that might exclude this type of study.

Longitudinal studies can be very expensive, particularly if the study is based in a laboratory. Researchers involved in a laboratory study might, for example, collect data every 6 months over a 3-year period. Therefore, it is easy to envisage costs being incurred in relation to the physiological equipment, consumables and transporting and communicating with all the subjects when testing is due. Of course, costs in longitudinal studies are substantially reduced if the design involves questionnaires. The Harvard alumni study, which has been longitudinally following graduates of Harvard University for the past 40 years and collecting data on lifestyle and health habits, have utilised this form of study to great effect.

The other potential disadvantage of a longitudinal study is that the longer the study goes on, the more likely you are to reduce your initial sample size. Subjects might move to a different area of the country and not respond to letters to be re-tested, become bored with the continual demands of the study, or develop other demands on their time, precluding their participation. The factors leading to subject mortality (see 'Threats to internal validity', p. 30) are known as attrition.

A third disadvantage and one that applies particularly to laboratory-based studies is that personnel may change from one year to the next, so that you will get a different person in charge of the test procedures, hence there is the potential for variance within the testing protocol. Therefore, it cannot be emphasised enough about the necessity for standardised procedures and the induction training of any new staff. Figure 3.2 presents a typical longitudinal design.

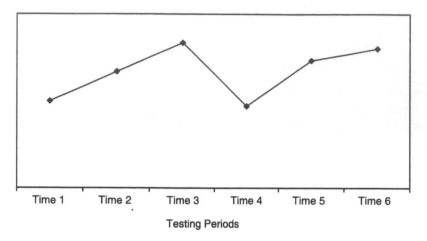

Testing Periods

Figure 3.2 Longitudinal design

True experimental

The true experiment is the strongest design for establishing causality because, providing the study has high internal validity, the researcher will have confidence that any differences observed in the dependent variable will be due to the manipulation of the independent variable. In sport and exercise science the true experiment is a very common design and one often used by undergraduate students. A student interested in the effects of a 6-week flexibility programme on quadriceps and hamstring flexibility would use the flexibility programme as the independent variable (sometimes referred to as the experimental or treatment variable). The dependent variable is the measurement of quadriceps and hamstring flexibility. In this scenario the undergraduate student also uses a comparison group, also known as a control group. All the participants are tested for flexibility of the quadriceps and hamstrings (known as the pre-test). The participants are then randomly assigned to either one group, which receives the new flexibility programme, or the control group, which continues with its normal daily routine. After 6 weeks all participants are re-tested (known as the post-test) and any differences between the two groups are noted. This structure of design is shown in Figure 3.3.

A serious threat to the internal validity of the two experiments would be the demoralisation of the control group once the groups learn that they are not getting the new form of flexibility training. An example of how to counter this would be to offer the control groups the chance to use the new form of aerobic training after the experiment is complete. In the event that the treatment is an ergogenic aid (e.g. creatine, carbohydrate solution, etc.), a similar substance in taste and appearance can be used as a placebo.

Other variations along this design can involve more than two groups or the use of a series of pre-tests before the independent variable is introduced followed by a series of post-tests. This design is known as an interrupted time series design. The major threat to the internal validity of any of these designs is to ensure that the groups are equivalent prior to the start of the manipulation of the independent variable. By randomly assigning them to one group or another, the researcher is increasing the chance of

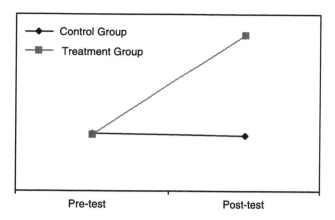

Figure 3.3 True experimental design

equivalence between the two groups. In the above flexibility scenario, the importance of equivalence between the two groups is vital for the dependent measure, flexibility. However, just by randomly assigning the participants into two groups does not necessarily mean they are equivalent. It is still possible that before the training begins, the treatment group will have greater or lesser flexibility when compared to the control group. This is a problem, because those with high flexibility are less likely to improve their flexibility as much as those who start with low flexibility.

One solution is to pre-test all participants first, then rank them in order of the most flexible first to the worst last. Next, randomly assign through the two highest ranked participants to either the training programme or the control group. This procedure is continued for the next ranked pair and the next until all are distributed into the two groups. This ensures that there is some equivalence on the dependent variable prior to the study starting.

Quasi-experimental

Quasi-experimental designs often cannot randomly assign subjects to treatment groups. Quasi-experimental designs are often used in educational research where non-equivalent control group design is frequently used. This means that equivalence between the two treatment groups could not be accomplished (Figure 3.4).

A key feature of the true experimental design (see p. 40) is that the researcher is able randomly to assign subjects to the experimental and control groups. However, random assignment is not always possible. With the flexibility training example, trying to randomly assign Olympic athletes to a treatment or a control group would be almost impossible as it is unlikely that any Olympic athlete would want to change their daily training routines. Therefore, where random assignment is not possible, these experiments are called quasi-experiments.

A common design in sport and exercise science is the non-equivalent control-group design. In this design the control group and the treatment group are pre-tested, the treatment group receive the manipulated independent variable and then both groups are post-tested, although none of the subjects is randomly assigned to the groups.

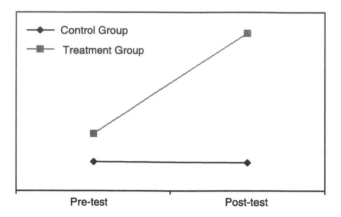

Figure 3.4 Quasi-experimental design

Whilst not as powerful as the true experimental, quasi-experiments are still useful, particularly when subject selection is a problem. However, if a difference is found between the pre-test and post-test scores of the treatment group, this finding is always suspect because it could be due to differences in one of the group characteristics and not the treatment effect.

A protocol that is often used in true experimental and quasi-experimental designs is that of the cross-over design. In this type of design the treatment group will first receive the manipulated independent variable whilst the control group will receive a placebo. After a certain amount of time, probably enough for the independent variable to show its effect on the dependent variables, the two group swap over or 'cross-over'. That is, the treatment group now becomes the control group whilst the control group now becomes the treatment group. This type of design has several opportunities. First, it will limit demoralisation of the control group as the subjects in the control group know that they too will receive the manipulated independent variable. Second, if the independent variable has the same effect not only on the first treatment group but also on the cross-over group, then the results are significantly stronger than just relying on one selected treatment group. Obviously, the design will provoke some interesting discussion if the cross-over causes one set of treatment results to be positive and the other set to be negative.

In some instances it is not possible to have a cross-over design and these often extend to studies using pharmacological drugs. This is due to the length of time that the physiological effects of the drugs stay in the body: usually there is a set time period before a different treatment can be enacted. In the early 1990s the effects of creatine supplementation were often assessed using a cross-over design until it was realised that a considerable number of days was required to wash out the creatine supplementation, meaning this design could no longer be used. If the design was used, it would mean that the first treatment group – if crossing over to the control group before all creatine supplement was washed out of the body – would still be affected by the treatment when supposedly acting as the control group.

Causal-comparative

The causal-comparative design is weaker than the previous two examples because it cannot confirm causality but can only be used as a guide. Thus, it is of most use as an exploratory design. The distinguishing feature of causal-comparative experiments is that groups of subjects might be compared that are different on a critical variable but are otherwise similar. For example, the British Olympic Association (BOA) is interested to determine what makes an Olympic champion. The BOA therefore decides to interview all British Olympians and to compare those who have won Olympic medals with those who have just failed to win a medal. The critical variable here is the winning of the medal but the athletes are essentially comparable in terms of representing their country, the comparable amounts of training, height, mass, etc. Clearly, a true experimental design would not be possible, but in this design possible causes of why some athletes are champions and others not could be identified. It would not be practical to manipulate athletes into winning situations for a gold medal or put them into situations whereby they just missed out, therefore the only alternative is to observe the effects as they happen naturally. This design is sometimes called *ex post facto*, because the causes are being studied after they have exerted their influence (e.g after the winning of a gold medal). Once the BOA have all the interview data, a number of issues might be raised. It might emerge that gold medal winners were athletes who were full-time whilst those just missing medals were part-time, or that access to facilities or sports science support were better. Owing to a variety of possible reasons, it is difficult to suggest what the causal factor may be. The major advantage is that the researcher is able to study cause and effect relationships, as they occur naturally in an athletic setting.

Correlational

A correlational study is the weakest design in which to conclude causality. The main purpose of correlational studies is to establish the strength of a relationship between two variables (see Chapter 6, p. 77). Although correlations cannot determine causality because they do not manipulate an independent variable, in a single study a large number of variables can be correlated against one another. This procedure is sometimes referred to as a scatter gun approach, whereby the researcher is unsure how the variables relate to one another. By measuring and then correlating variables against one another, significant variables may emerge, focusing further investigations. Conversely, insignificant correlations may suggest that there is nothing to be gained from exploring these relationships further, thereby saving the researcher time and expense on additional studies.

Undergraduate students often make the mistake of concluding causality from correlations, but this is not the most common misunderstanding. The most common misunderstanding arises when a student fails to acknowledge that any relationship between two variables could be the result of a third, as yet unmeasured, variable. For example, there is a strong correlation between $\dot{V}O_2$ max and running performance. However, $\dot{V}O_2$ max is just one correlate to running performance and linked to it are such variables as the lactate threshold value, the maximal running speed at $\dot{V}O_2$ max, and the maximal lactate steady state. In addition, correlation studies are dependent on the sample population. In a group of runners with a wide range of abilities (referred to as a

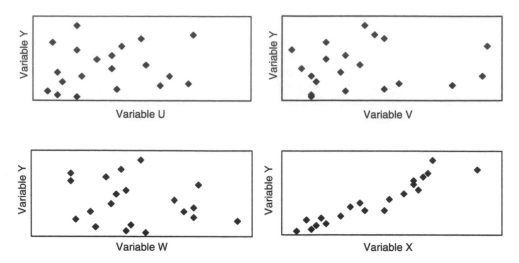

Figure 3.5 Correlational design

heterogeneous group), the correlation between running performance and $\dot{V}O_2$ max will be stronger than for a group of runners with very similar running abilities (a homogeneous group). This is because the homogeneous runners will have similar $\dot{V}O_2$ max scores but the runners will not all finish the race first; therefore, there must be some other distinguishing factor that accounts for the difference in running performance. Consequently, when examining correlational studies, the sample population group should always be noted for whether it is a homogeneous or heterogeneous group.

The main advantages of correlational studies are that they are easier to organise than true experiments, do not require detailed statistical analyses, and provide data with which to consider a more detailed study. The main weaknesses are the absence of concluding causality and the interrelationships between many variables.

Selecting the appropriate experimental design

Once you have formulated your research hypothesis, you should consider into what design category your hypothesis fits. A number of simple questions should help answer the problem:

1 Is your hypothesis searching for a cause and effect?
2 Does your hypothesis manipulate the independent variable?
3 Is there a random assignment of groups or subjects?
4 Does your hypothesis create variation in the dependent variable?
5 Does the hypothesis try to establish or explain some pre-existing relationship in the dependent variable?
6 Does the experiment repeatedly (twice or more) measure the same subjects on the same variable (a repeated measures design)?

By using Table 3.1, you should be able to conclude what type of research design your hypothesis belongs to. Once a decision is taken about the design, it is straightforward to

Table 3.1 The differences in the four types of research design

	Research design			
	Experimental	Quasi-experimental	Causal-comparative	Correlational
Establishes cause and effect	✓	✓	✓	✗
Manipulates independent variable	✓	✓	✗	✗
Random assignment	✓	✗	✗	✗
Creates variation in dependent variable	✓	✓	✗	✗
Tries to explain pre-existing relationship in dependent variable	✗	✗	✓	✓
Repeated measures	✓	✓	✗	✗

determine the type of design protocol that will allow you to answer your question. The acceptance of a particular design will also allow you to consider the threats to the internal validity of the experiment and how you might best control for these threats.

SUMMARY

Kerlinger (1986) states that relations are the essence of science and that research design is vitally important if causal relationships are to be found. The design of any research serves two purposes. First, it provides answers to research questions and, second, it attempts to control variance. When an answer to a research question is obtained, its acceptance by other researchers will only happen if extraneous variables have been controlled (Figure 3.6). If this is not the case, then other plausible explanations could have caused the effect.

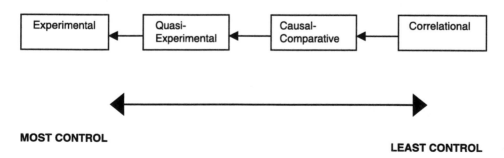

Figure 3.6 Schematic representing the confidence to conclude causality

The main technical function of research design is to be able to control variance. The control involves two factors:

1   To eliminate plausible alternative explanations so that other sources of variance do not distort the relationships between the specified variables.
2   To control the source of variance that affects the dependent variable.

In order to control the variance, the researcher must control extraneous variance and minimise the error variance. Only if the researcher is confident that they are able to do this can they have confidence in their conclusion of a cause and effect relationship.

The type of research design a student chooses is dependent upon the degree to which causal conclusions are important. In experimental research designs the researcher will manipulate one or more variables whilst attempting to control other variables. This allows for the strongest possibility of drawing causal conclusions. Correlational research designs make no attempt to draw causal conclusions but examine how strongly two variables are related to each other. Causal-comparative research is somewhere in the middle of the above two cited examples in that it attempts to stimulate an experiment by examining two groups who are similar in every way but one.

4

AVERAGES AND DISTRIBUTION

> Statistics, the science that states if you have your feet in the freezer and
> your head in the oven, on average you are warm.
>
> Anon

LEARNING OUTCOMES

Following this chapter you should be able to:

1   calculate and interpret different measures of central tendency (averages);
2   calculate and interpret different measures of group variance;
3   distinguish between different patterns of data distribution.

Prior to reading this section you should be familiar with the following terms:

* average
* variance
* distribution
* frequency.

Introduction

'Average' is a term that has numerous meanings. It is most commonly used to reflect
something that is ordinary or run of the mill. If you ask someone how their meal was,
and they reply that 'it was average', you infer that it was neither the best meal they have
eaten, nor the worst. In fact, this tells you it was somewhere in the middle of their
culinary experiences. This is essentially the same as the mathematical meaning of average, where we are interested in the centre point of our data. Mathematically speaking,
there are three main ways in which to determine the centre point, or average of data.
These are the mean, the median and the mode. You are probably fairly familiar with
calculating these different averages, but may be less familiar with interpreting them.
These three figures will rarely be exactly the same: the way they interrelate can tell you
some very important things about data you have collected.

Why are people so concerned with averages? Well, imagine that you are taking an
exam for one of your courses and you are told that your score is above average for the
group. How would you feel? Quite pleased with yourself?

Now imagine that you are told that your score was miscalculated and actually you are
below average for the group. Not quite so pleased with yourself now? This highlights
the first purpose of an average, to compare individual scores (i.e. your score) against the

centre point of the group. This allows us to view each data point (i.e. each student) relative to the whole group.

Donald Bradman, an Australian cricketer, played a total of 80 test matches. His test match batting average was 99.94. In this instance we are using an average to summarise a group. The group in this case consists of every test match innings that Donald Bradman had. The average 99.94 tells us that over this group of innings he tended to score very highly. The use of an average to summarise a group is the second main use of an average. This allows us to make easy comparisons between different groups.

For example, if we wanted to examine differences between the sensation-seeking scores for a group of team sport players and a group of extreme sports participants, we would tend to look at the averages of both groups to make a comparison. When summarising a group or comparing two or more groups, it is usual to look at average data.

Different types of averages

The most commonly used average is the arithmetic mean. Table 4.1 shows the height of children in a particular year group in a school. The mean has been calculated by summing all children's heights and dividing this figure by the number of children in the year group. The median has been calculated by highlighting which number is the central number, when all scores in the group are arranged in numerical order (when there are an even number of scores, and therefore two central numbers, the mean of the two central numbers is taken). The mode was established by finding the most frequently occurring score.

The data in Table 4.1 lead to the three averages being very close to one another. In these circumstances the purpose of calculating all three averages is difficult to understand. It is easier to see the purpose of the three different averages when we relate them to a distribution curve. A distribution curve shows the pattern produced by the frequency of the scores. The first step in producing a distribution curve is to produce a grouped frequency table. Table 4.2 is a grouped frequency table for the height data for the year group. Essentially this shows us how many times scores occur within certain ranges. For example, three children have a height of between 122 and 124 cm.

From a grouped frequency table, we can construct a frequency histogram (Figure 4.1). On a frequency histogram the x axis represents the variable in which we are examining the distribution (e.g. height) and the y axis represents the frequency of

Table 4.1 Raw scores for height (cm) of a year group of children

120	128	132	134	135	138	141	147
122	129	132	134	136	139	142	148
123	130	133	134	136	139	142	148
123	130	133	135	136	139	143	149
125	131	133	135	137	139	144	150
125	131	133	135	137	139	144	151
126	131	133	135	137	140	145	Mean
127	132	134	135*+	138	140	145	=
128	132	134	135	138	141	146	135.8

* = median   + = mode

Table 4.2 Grouped frequency table for
height of a year group of children

Height (cm)	Frequency
119–121	1
122–124	3
125–127	4
128–130	5
131–133	12
134–136	15
137–139	11
140–142	6
143–145	5
146–148	4
149–151	3

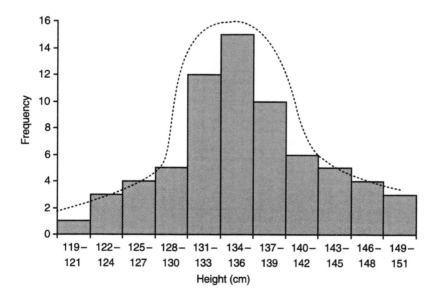

Figure 4.1 Frequency histogram for height of a year group of children

occurrence within the group we are examining (e.g. the year group). A smoothed curve following the histogram gives us the distribution curve Figure 4.1.

When we examine the three averages in relation to the distribution curve, we can see that for our height data, all the averages lie at the apex of the curve, which is located at the centre of the curve. The distribution curve produced by this data is symmetrical and bell shaped, this shape is referred to as a normal distribution curve.

Normal distribution

A normal distribution curve shows the pattern of normally distributed data. Sir Francis Galton (1822–1911), a cousin of Charles Darwin, was the first scientist to introduce the concept of normal distribution, which is an important concept in all the natural sciences. However, his reputation is now somewhat tarnished following his later study into eugenics, where he investigated racial differences in characteristics such as intelligence. Normal distribution is sometimes referred to as Gaussian distribution, named after the brilliant German mathematician and astronomer Karl Friedrich Gauss (1777–1855), who applied the concept of normal distribution to analyse astronomical data.

Normal distribution is the most important type of distribution in statistics for two reasons:

1   Normal distribution occurs naturally in many types of data, from physical characteristics (e.g. body mass), to performance scores (e.g. 3000-metre running time), to psychological characteristics (e.g. state anxiety score).
2   Many statistical tests (some of which will be covered in later chapters), referred to as parametric statistical tests, assume that the data being analysed are normally distributed. If these tests are carried out on data that are not normally distributed, then this assumption is violated. This affects the validity of the results obtained from these statistical tests.

The first point is really just an extension of a principle of common sense that you probably already feel familiar with. This is the idea that the most common score for a measure, in a group of people, is likely to be around the average score. Further, the frequency distribution around this average will follow the bell-shaped pattern. If you think about the height data in our example, the most common height range is 134–136 cm for our group of children. Fewer children are in the range below this (131–133 cm), or the range above this (137–139 cm). As we get further away from the most common range (at the centre of the curve), we get fewer and fewer children located within this range. You are probably able to come up with numerous common-sense examples of where this same pattern occurs. However, normal distribution extends beyond common sense, in that we are able to predict what percentage of people will fall within given ranges, through using a statistic called the standard deviation (see p. 55). This is possible for normally distributed data, which is the most common form of distribution, however there are types of distribution which are classified as non-normal.

Skewness

For example, what if we had included within our data set the sports teachers and teaching assistants from this year? Table 4.3 shows the addition of the adults' heights to the data set. Figure 4.2 displays the distribution histogram and curve for the sample now. You can see that we now have an asymmetric curve, which we refer to as being skewed. In this instance the data are positively skewed, because the tail of the data is skewed above (positive) the curve.

From Table 4.3 it is possible to see that the pattern of the three averages has changed. Whereas with the normally distributed data (excluding the adults' heights) the three averages were very similar, now the mean is the highest figure, followed by the median, with the mode being the lowest figure. This is a characteristic of positively skewed data. Negatively skewed data, where the tail of the data is skewed below (negative) the curve, will show the opposite relationship between the different averages (see Figure 4.3). The mode will usually be higher than the median, which in turn will be higher than the mean.

Table 4.3 Raw scores for height (cm) of a year group of children and their teachers and assistants

120	128	132	134	135	138	141	147	**175**
122	129	132	134	136*	139	142	148	**179**
123	130	133	134	136	139	142	148	**181**
123	130	133	135	136	139	143	149	
125	131	133	135	137	139	144	150	
125	131	133	135	137	139	144	151	**Mean**
126	131	133	135	137	140	145	**162**	=
127	132	134	135+	138	140	145	**167**	**138.8**
128	132	134	135	138	141	146	**174**	

* = median   + = mode   **bold** denotes adult score

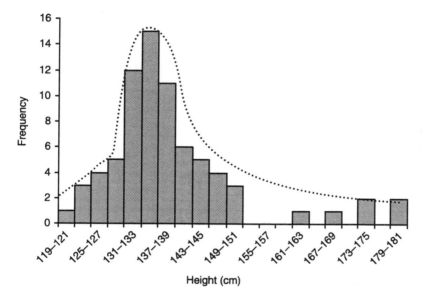

Figure 4.2 Frequency histogram for height of a year group of children and their teachers and assistants

Thus, through observing the distribution curve and checking the order and proximity of the three averages, we can get a sense of whether the data are skewed. Skewness can, however, be calculated statistically. Amongst the descriptive statistics SPSS (Statistical Package for the Social Sciences) is able to calculate, is a value for skewness (see Chapter 3 of Coakes and Steed [2001] for more details). If the skewness value is positive, the data are positively skewed, and if the figure is negative, the data are negatively skewed. A figure of zero indicates that the data are not skewed. However, data are almost always slightly skewed in one direction, therefore the researcher needs to make a decision about whether the level of skewness is acceptable.

With the height data for the children alone, we obtain a skewness value of 0.07, indicating a minute amount of positive skewness. When we take the data set, with the adult heights added, the skewness value increases to 1.76, showing that the positive skewness of the data has increased with this addition. The skewness value itself is difficult to interpret. In order to decide whether the amount of skewness present is

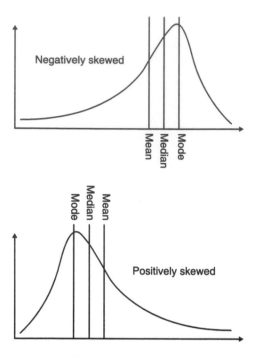

Figure 4.3 Skewed distribution curves with different averages

acceptable, we have to divide the skewness value by the standard error for skewness (Equation 4.1). In effect, this corrects for the number of subjects in our data set. The more subjects there are, the lower the standard error will be. Thus the standard error for the children alone is 0.29, but for the children and the adults it decreases to 0.28. We base the decision on skewness upon the standardised skewness score calculated through Equation 4.1. If the standardised skewness score is greater than ±2 then the level of skewness is unacceptable and the data are considered to have a non-normal distribution. In calculating the standardised skewness scores for the height data, we can see that the children in isolation produce a figure below 2 (Equation 4.1). With the adult data added to the children's data, a score above 3 is produced, indicating that the data are sufficiently positively skewed to be regarded as non-normal.

Equation 4.1

$$\text{Standardised skewness} = \frac{\text{Skewness}}{\text{Standard error for skewness}}$$

$$\begin{array}{l}\text{Standardised skewness} \\ \text{(for children alone)}\end{array} = \frac{0.07}{0.29} = 0.31$$

$$\begin{array}{l}\text{Standardised skewness} \\ \text{(for children and adults)}\end{array} = \frac{1.76}{0.28} = 6.29$$

Multimodal data

Supposing we continued to collect height data on these children, in order to investigate changes in height throughout adolescence. Figure 4.4 shows the distribution curve and histogram for the same group of children when they reach 18 years of age.

It can be seen that there are two peaks to the graph. This pattern is referred to as a bimodal distribution (meaning that two modes exist). Although strictly speaking there may be only a single mode average present within the data, the appearance of two distinct peaks to the distribution curve is still referred to as bimodal. In this example, the two peaks are centred around 167–169 cm and 176–178 cm. What do you think accounts for the bimodalism present in this data? Why might it occur in the adult data, but not in the childhood data? Try to answer this question before reading on.

The answer relates to gender: adult men tend to be taller than women, and thus men cluster around a higher mode than women. The approximately equal split between genders means that the distribution curve will show two peaks, one relating to the mode for men, the other relating to the mode for women. In this instance the mean and the median will fall between these two modes. The occurrence of more than one peak in the distribution curve is often indicative of the existence of two distribution curves within the data. Each distribution curve may represent a different sub-group within the overall group (e.g. males and females).

Gender is a frequent source of bimodalism when analysing anthropometric or physical performance data, from a mixed gender sample of adults. However, other factors can also account for multimodalism (more than one mode). Examples might include distinct age groups being included in the data set, or different standards or types of athletes being incorporated into the same data set. The peaks within the distribution curve are unlikely to be all exactly the same height, thus technically only one mode may exist within the data. Nevertheless the data are still referred to as multimodal, because each peak potentially represents the mode of a sub-group. The height of each peak will

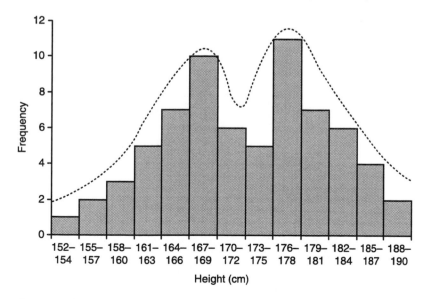

Figure 4.4 Frequency histogram for group of 18-year-olds

represent the proportion of subjects within the corresponding sub-group. Therefore, height data for a mixed gender group are likely to possess two equal sized peaks because of the equal proportion of males and females.

The occurrence of multimodalism may require you to split the group into separate sub-groups, so that analysis can be carried out on each sub-group separately. Its presence may be the first indication that the group you are investigating has sub-groups within it. You might then have to look at all your data more closely to try to understand why these groups differ on your dependent variable.

Variance

In examining the vertical ground reaction force produced during the take-off phase of a long jump, what would you think would be the major differences between a group of elite jumpers and a group taken at random from the population?

The first difference you would think of would probably be that the ground reaction forces of the elite jumpers would be much higher than those of the other group. How about the spread of results within each group? The elite group would all be a similar mass, be travelling at a similar velocity, and be using a similar technique: this would lead to similar ground reaction forces being produced. The randomly selected group, however, would contain people of different ages, mass and jumping experience. It would be possible to have a young, well-conditioned subject with some previous jumping experience in the group, as well as a sedentary 70-year-old who has never done the long jump. The result would be that the randomly selected group would probably have a much greater spread of scores for this variable (ground reaction force). Groups with little spread, where the scores all cluster closely to one another, are referred to as homogeneous (*homo* = same, *genos* = kind). A group where the scores are completely spread out is referred to as heterogeneous (*hetero* = different, *genos* = kind). The spread of the data is termed the variance.

Measures of variance

Range

Table 4.4 shows the reaction time scores for eight university first team cricket players and eight sedentary age-matched university students, to a cricket specific stimulus.

Table 4.4 Reaction time data for cricketers and non-cricketers

Reaction time for cricketers (s)	*Reaction time for non-cricketers (s)*
0.47	0.55
0.49	0.59
0.49	0.64
0.51	0.71
0.52	0.73
0.55	0.77
0.56	0.82
0.58	0.84

The range is calculated by reporting the lowest and highest score for the group. The range is therefore 0.47–0.58 s for the cricket players and 0.55–0.84 s for the sedentary students. The range provides two pieces of information:

1   *An indication of the variance of the data.* In this instance we can see that the university cricket players (0.58 − 0.47 = 0.11 s) are more homogeneous than the sedentary students (0.84 − 0.55 = 0.29 s).
2   *A summary of the relatives scores of a group.* With our reaction time data we are able to determine that the cricket players' reaction times for this task are quicker than the sedentary group.

The range is advantageous because it informs us about the variance of a group and summarises the group's scores. The major benefit of the range is its ease of calculation. The problem with the range is that it can easily be distorted by a single score within the group. For example, the inclusion of a cricket player with a reaction time of 0.98 s for the task would change the range for this group to 0.47–0.98 s. This would give the appearance that this group is more heterogeneous (0.98 − 0.47 = 0.51 s) than the sedentary students. The cricket players would also then appear to possess slower reaction times than the sedentary group. The introduction of a single piece of data can influence the range greatly, even though the underlying characteristics of the group have not really changed that much.

Standard deviation

The standard deviation was first used in 1893 by the British mathematician Karl Pearson. Pearson's work followed on from the work of Gauss and Galton; this link was continued by Pearson being appointed the first Galton Professor of Eugenics, at University College, London. He was interested in looking at the way normally distributed data varied. He devised the standard deviation to give an indication of the average amount that each score within a group varied from the mean.

Table 4.5 shows data for the women's 100-metre final at an elite international competition. Eight runners took part in the final and their data are listed in order of their placings (fastest first). The table shows the working out for each of the six steps used to calculate the standard deviation.

Equation 4.2

The six steps to calculating the standard deviation for a population are listed below:

1   Calculate the mean of the data $\bar{X}$

2   Calculate how much each data point deviates from the mean $X - \bar{X}$

    These numbers may be positives or negatives.

3   Square each of these deviations $(X - \bar{X})^2$

    This makes all the deviations positive (but we will have to square root them later to reduce them to their original value).

4   Sum (add together) all the squared deviations $\Sigma(X - \bar{X})^2$

5   Divide this figure by the number of scores in the group $\dfrac{\Sigma(X - \bar{X})^2}{n}$

This gives us the average squared deviation within the population.

6   Square root this figure $\sigma = \sqrt{\dfrac{\Sigma(X - \bar{X})^2}{n}}$

This gives us the average amount that each score deviates from the mean. This is known as the standard deviation and the formula following step 6 is the formula for calculating the standard deviation of a population.

Table 4.5 Standard deviation calculations for women's 100 metre times

Runner	100 m time (s) X	$X - \bar{X}$	$(X - \bar{X})^2$
1	11.01	−0.14	0.0196
2	11.07	−0.08	0.0064
3	11.09	−0.06	0.0036
4	11.12	−0.03	0.0009
5	11.13	−0.02	0.0004
6	11.21	0.06	0.0036
7	11.25	0.1	0.01
8	11.32	0.17	0.0289
Mean $\bar{X}$	11.15	$\Sigma(X - \bar{X})^2$	**0.0734**

$\Sigma(X - \bar{X})^2 = 0.0734$

$\dfrac{\Sigma(X - \bar{X})^2}{n}$

$= \dfrac{0.0734}{n} = \dfrac{0.0734}{8} = 0.0092$

$\sqrt{\dfrac{\Sigma(X - \bar{X})^2}{n}} = \sqrt{0.0092} = \mathbf{0.1}$

The value for standard deviation is given in the units that the measurements are recorded in. It is reported as plus or minus (±) and represents the average amount that scores within a population deviate above or below the mean. With our 100 metre sprint time data, the standard deviation is ±0.1 s, indicating that on average the sprinters in this population will be above or below the mean score (11.15 s) by 0.1 s.

The formula provided above for calculating the standard deviation relates to a population. On most occasions it is impractical to collect data from every member of a population, as the number contained within populations is usually very large. In this instance we normally collect data from a section of the population. This section of the population is referred to as a sample. The data from the sample is often used to reflect the population as a whole. The process of drawing conclusions about the population, based upon the sample data, is called statistical inference. We often calculate the standard deviation of a sample to give an estimate of variance within the population from which it was drawn. In small samples bias affects this estimate; in order to compensate for this bias following formula is used:

$$SD = \sqrt{\frac{\Sigma(X - \overline{X})^2}{n - 1}}$$

Generally, σ (the Greek letter sigma) is used as a symbol for the population standard deviation, and SD is used to represent the sample standard deviation. You are likely to be most commonly analysing data from samples and therefore using the SD formula, but it is important to become familiar with when to use each formula.

Coefficient of variation

One limitation of the standard deviation is that because it is calculated in the measurement units used for each individual variable, it is difficult to make comparisons between different variables. For instance, does a standard deviation for height, of ±7.9 cm, represent greater variance than a standard deviation for body mass, of ±4.6 kg?

The coefficient of variation (CV) is a way of expressing the standard deviation relative to the mean (as a percentage). It is calculated through the following equation:

Equation 4.3

$$CV = \left(\frac{SD}{MEAN}\right) \times 100$$

The CV enables the researcher to compare the variance of data measured in different units. However, it is influenced by large discrepancies in the size of the mean. For example, a researcher wishing to know the variance of measurements produced by a set of scales may weigh a standard weight on several occasions. If they had weighed a 50 kg weight and discovered a standard deviation of ±0.5 kg, they would have calculated a CV of 1 per cent and may have concluded that the scales were fairly reliable. However, if they had used a 5 kg weight and obtained the same standard deviation of ±0.5 kg, they would have found a CV of 10 per cent instead and drawn a different conclusion about the reliability of the scales.

Standard deviation and the normal distribution

The area beneath a normal distribution curve corresponds to 100 per cent of the group represented by the curve (i.e. every member of the group's score is included). Because the peak of the curve represents the highest frequency of occurrence, the area around the centre of the curve contains a greater percentage of the population than the extremities of the curve (Figure 4.5).

With a normal distribution curve, the percentage of the group contained in certain sectors of the curve can be accurately estimated, because of the predictable shape of the curve. These predictions are based around the mean and the standard deviation. Figure 4.5 shows that approximately 68 per cent of the group is located one standard deviation either side of the mean. Because of the symmetry of the normal curve, this means that 16 per cent of the group are contained in the area above one standard deviation, and 16 per cent of the group are included in the area below

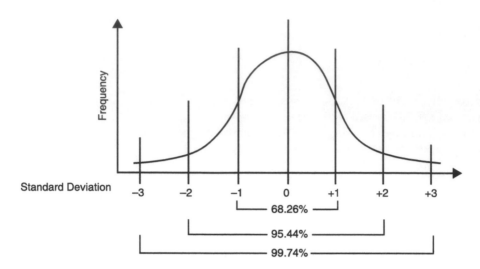

Figure 4.5 Normal distribution curve

one standard deviation. Consequently, someone scoring over two standard deviations above the mean would be in approximately the top 2.5 per cent of the population ($100 - 95\% = 5\%$, $5\% \div 2 = 2.5\%$).

This predictability relating to the percentage of a group falling within a certain sector of the distribution curve is referred to as mesokurtosis (*mesos* = middle, *kurtosis* = bulging). There is a particular type of non-normality where the spread of the scores within the group does not follow this pattern (Figure 4.6). With some data a greater

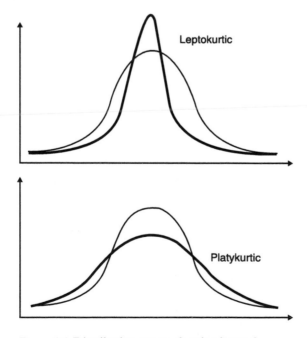

Figure 4.6 Distribution curves showing kurtosis

percentage falls at the extremities of the distribution curve, and not as much is located at the centre. This is called platykurtosis (*platus* = flat, *kurtosis* = bulging) because of the flatter appearance of the curve. The opposite situation involves a greater concentration of the data close to the centre of the curve, and less at the extremities of the curve. This is called leptokurtosis (*lepto* = thin, *kurtosis* = bulging), referring to the pointed nature of the curve.

As with skewness, kurtosis can be measured statistically. If the value is negative, the data are leptokurtic. A positive score indicates platykurtic data, and a score of zero reflects perfect mesokurtosis. Perfect mesoskurtosis is rare and so some way of determining the acceptability of the extent of the leptokurtosis or platykurtosis is required. This is achieved through Equation 4.4, which is similar to the equation used to calculate standardised skewness (Equation 4.1). The constituents of this equation can be calculated through the descriptive statistics produced by SPSS (see Coakes and Steed 2001). A standardised kurtosis score above ±2 is considered to reflect non-normality.

Equation 4.4

$$\text{Standardised Kurtosis} = \frac{\text{Kurtosis}}{\text{Standard error for Kurtosis}}$$

SUMMARY

Measures of central tendency and variance are the first step to understanding your data as a collection of scores. Before more complicated analyses are performed, it is advisable to perform these rudimentary analyses first. Averages will allow you to compare groups against one another and look at individual scores within the context of the group. By doing this you will start to see whether differences are present between groups. Measures of variance will give you information about the spread of the group. This will enable you to understand the composition of the group. Understanding the distribution, and whether it is normal, will help you to decide what tests to use when you come to use more sophisticated analyses.

While conclusions about your data should not be drawn from these descriptive procedures alone, they can allow you to start to see patterns in your data. The following questions can be used to help you to gain an initial understanding of the data:

1   Examine the means of any experimental groups. Are there differences between the means? What might account for this?
2   Look at individual scores relative to the means. Are any members of the group a long way away from the group mean? Is there anything different about these subjects?
3   Having examined the different measures of variance, would you describe your group as homogeneous, heterogeneous, or balanced between these two characteristics?
4   How would you describe the distribution of the data? Is it normally distributed? If not, in what way is it non-normal?

5

STATISTICAL TESTS OF DIFFERENCE

[T]he cause of science may be prejudiced far more gravely in the long run by the erroneous, and perhaps permanent abandonment of a true H(1). By its very nature the incorrect rejection of H(0) invites ultimate exposure. Type II error, however, is more likely to escape detection.

Miller and Knapp (1971)

LEARNING OUTCOMES

Following this chapter you should be able to:

1 identify when it is appropriate to use a statistical test of difference and select the correct test to use;
2 describe what constitutes a type I and type II error, within the context of a test of difference;
3 interpret the results of a range of statistical tests of difference.

Prior to this section you should be familiar with the following terms:

- hypothesis
- sample
- normal distribution.

Introduction

One of the most commonly used types of statistical test is a test of difference. This is required when a researcher is investigating whether two or more groups are different from one another in a particular characteristic (the dependent variable). The focus might be hamstring flexibility in males and females. In this instance the investigator would be trying to detect differences between males and females (two different groups) in hamstring flexibility (a particular characteristic). The alternate hypothesis would state that there *would* be a difference in hamstring flexibility between males and females. The null hypothesis would state there *would not* be a difference in hamstring flexibility between males and females.

The groups are categorised based upon the independent variable, which in this example is gender. The dependent variable is the characteristic that is being measured, which would be hamstring flexibility, perhaps measured in cm as with a sit and reach test, or degrees range of motion during a straight leg raise. It is referred to as the dependent variable because the alternate hypothesis supposes that it *depends* upon the independent variable. In other words, if the alternate hypothesis is correct, hamstring flexibility depends upon the gender of an individual.

It is usual for statistical inference (see 'Standard deviation', p. 55) to be employed when using a test of difference. It is obviously impossible to measure the hamstring flexibility of every male and every female in existence. So instead we measure a sample of males and a sample of females (perhaps 50 males and 50 females), and make inferences about the whole population based upon the scores within each sample. The main statistics that we are interested in are the means of each sample and some measure of variance (see p. 54) within each sample. The researcher is trying to determine whether the difference between the two means is large enough to reflect a real difference between the two populations from which the samples are drawn.

You might think that any difference in the means of the two samples would reflect a difference between the two populations from which the samples were drawn. For example, the mean hamstring flexibility of the 50 males, as measured by a straight leg raise, might be 92.5 degrees (Figure 5.1). The mean for the 50 females might be 94.8 degrees (Figure 5.1). You might be prepared to take this as evidence that females have greater hamstring flexibility than males.

However, two samples drawn from the same population (rather than different populations) are unlikely to possess exactly the same means. If we were to measure the hamstring flexibility of another sample of 50 different females, it is unlikely that the mean of this sample will also be exactly 94.8 degrees. Imagine that the mean for this new sample was 91.6 degrees (Figure 5.2). What would you now conclude about gender and hamstring flexibility? Are females more flexible than males? Are females less flexible than males? Is there no difference in flexibility between females and males?

The solution to these questions is very difficult to answer and is the main reason that statistical tests are used to test for difference. They help the researcher to reach an objective decision about the data they have collected. The primary issue that makes it difficult to interpret this type of data is that samples drawn from the same population

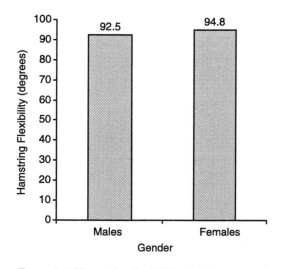

Figure 5.1 Hamstring flexibility of different genders

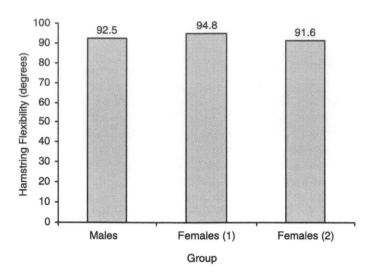

Figure 5.2 Differences in hamstring flexibility between samples from the same population

may have different means. If this is the case, it becomes very difficult to judge differences between means of samples drawn from different populations.

The reason that samples obtained from the same population may have different means is due to the variance within that population. If variance did not exist in a population (i.e. it was perfectly homogeneous), then the means from repeat samples would always be identical. Were everybody within a population of identical body fat percentage, then no matter how many samples you drew from this population, the means would always be the same. However, in the real world members of a population will have a range of body fat percentages; this variance means that two samples selected from this one population are likely to possess different means for fat percentage. We will refer to these differences in the means of two samples randomly selected from the same population as chance differences. Equation 5.1 shows the mean body fat percentage scores of two different samples each consisting of 10 adults randomly selected from the general population.

Equation 5.1

17.6 (sample 1 mean) − 16.1 (sample 2 mean) = 1.5%

In Equation 5.1, the mean of sample 1 is slightly higher (17.6 per cent) than the mean of sample 2 (16.1 per cent). The difference between these two groups is therefore 1.5 per cent. If we were to select and measure two more samples, the size of the difference between the means would be unlikely to be exactly 1.5 per cent. In this case the sample 1 mean might be slightly lower than the sample 2 mean, giving us a negative number. We could go on selecting and measuring pairs of samples from this population thousands of times. This would give us thousands of scores for chance differences between means. We can think of these scores as forming a hypothetical population of scores representing the chance differences between means. Provided all our samples were randomly selected, this hypothetical population would possess an interesting characteristic. It would be normally distributed and would have a mean of zero (Figure 5.3). This makes intuitive sense, as sometimes we would get a positive difference, sometimes a negative difference, but overall on average the difference would be zero. Also, we would expect most differences between the means to be small and close to zero (the centre of the distribution curve). Fewer differences would be large and at the edges of the distribution curve. This 'population of chance differences' would also have a standard deviation, and we could use this to tell us what percentage of the population falls within certain ranges. We call this standard deviation the standard error of the difference (SE_D). This is useful because, if you remember back to Chapter 4, we showed that in a normally distributed population, we could say 68 per cent of the population lay within one standard deviation either side of the mean, 95.44 per cent lay within two standard deviations, etc. We are therefore able to say that ~95 per cent of these chance differences fall within two standard deviations either side of the mean of zero. In other words ~95 per cent of the chance differences will fall within $2SE_D$ either side of zero.

For hamstring flexibility in females, the standard error of the difference (the standard deviation for these chance differences) might be 1.8 degrees. This would mean 95 per cent of the chance differences would lie between −3.6 and +3.6 degrees (two standard deviations either side of the mean of zero). Now, let us return to the reason behind this examination of chance differences, that is the measurement of non-chance differences, i.e. looking for differences in the means of different populations. If we wanted to determine whether there was a difference in the hamstring flexibility of females when compared with males, we could randomly select a sample of males and a sample of females. If the differences between the means of these two samples is greater than ±3.6 degrees, we would know that there was only a 5 per cent chance that this size of difference could occur by chance. We know this because 95 per cent of the chance difference lies within ±3.6 degrees, therefore only 5 per cent can lie outside of it. If the difference were greater than this and we declared that there was a difference between hamstring flexibility for males and females (our original alternate hypothesis), then we

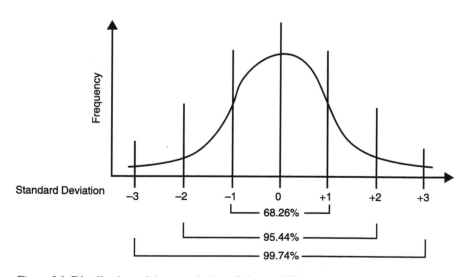

Figure 5.3 Distribution of the population of chance differences

would have only a 5 per cent chance of being wrong. Accepting the alternative hypothesis as true when it is actually false is referred to as a type I error. Thus, in these circumstances the probability of making a type I error would be 5 per cent (or 0.05). This approach allows the investigator to compare the actual difference observed between two samples from different populations, with the chance differences that would occur by selecting two samples from the same population. The lower the probability that the observed size of difference could have occurred by chance, the more certain the investigator can be that there is a genuine difference between the populations. Although theoretically any size of difference may occur between samples by chance, large differences are much less likely to occur through chance alone. Therefore, a researcher can say that they will only accept that there is a genuine difference, if there is a less than a certain probability (e.g. 5 per cent) that it could have occurred by chance.

Although this fundamental idea about chance differences forms the basis of most statistical tests of difference, in the real world of data collection it would be very difficult to collect thousands of pairs of samples from the same population. Therefore a measure of the variance of the scores within each real sample taken from a different population is used to estimate the parameters relating to the population of differences. For example, to estimate the standard error of the difference for hamstring flexibility in samples of females (i.e. the differences between the means of samples drawn from the same population of females), a measure of variance from the actual sample of 50 females would be used. The larger the variance within the sample, the greater the likelihood of larger differences occurring by chance. A sample drawn from a population that shows high variance would suggest that the population from which it is drawn is going to possess high variance. High variance in the sample for hamstring flexibility suggests that women in general possess a wide range of scores for flexibility. You are likely to get women with very good flexibility and women with very limited flexibility. Consequently, samples drawn from this population are more likely to vary by larger amounts. One sample could be composed of those with lower flexibility, whereas another sample might contain women with high flexibility. Lower variance in the sample that is actually measured means these larger differences are less likely to occur by chance. Fewer women would exist who were at the extremes of the flexibility spectrum, thus there would be less chance of samples being heavily weighted. In an extreme example where no variance existed, with every woman possessing an identical hamstring flexibility, the chance of any two samples being different would be zero.

Type I and type II errors

As previously mentioned, a researcher can make mistakes when accepting or rejecting hypotheses. In particular, there are two types of mistake with which a researcher is concerned. We have already mentioned the first of these, which is referred to as a type I error, or an alpha (α) error. Type I errors involve the acceptance of the alternate hypothesis when the null hypothesis is actually correct. In a test of difference this means declaring there is a difference between samples, when in fact none exists. It is analogous to declaring a defendant guilty when they are in fact innocent. In most experimental designs where a test of difference is used, accepting the alternate hypothesis usually has greater ramifications than accepting the null hypothesis. It may mean that a treatment group is judged to be different from a control group, the implication being that the treatment is effective in causing the difference between the groups. It could be that two populations, for example ethnic groups, are considered to be different in some aspect of human performance. Whatever the conclusion, it often leads to a change in behaviour (e.g. the use of a new treatment), or perception (e.g. one ethnic group being viewed as superior to others in certain characteristics). The implications may be contentious, or have serious repercussions if the conclusions are subsequently found to be false. The scientific method has evolved to be cautious in the acceptance of new findings (see Chapter 1).

As a result of this paradigm, researchers are always acutely aware of the probability of making a type I error. One of the primary foci of most scientists using statistical tests is what is the chance of making a type I error, similar to a jury considering the chance of making a wrongful conviction. In the field of sport and exercise science, a value of 0.05 for the probability of making a type I error is usually selected as a threshold for accepting the alternate hypothesis. This means there is less than a 5 per cent (or 1 in 20) chance of declaring a difference, when no true difference exists. Any measured difference between samples which is large enough for there to be less than a 5 per cent probability of it being a chance difference is declared a significant difference. This value of 0.05 is often called a p value (p for probability), or an alpha level (as in alpha error). Experiments where the consequences of committing a type I error may lead to a risk to human health, or a large waste of money and resources, may use a more conservative threshold of 0.01 (1 in 100) or even 0.001 (1 in 1,000). However, recently there has been a trend within sport and exercise science to move away from the use of arbitrary probability thresholds (see Chapter 9). Instead of drawing a line in the sand at a given probability and then accepting or rejecting a hypothesis based upon whether the p value crosses that line, the probability of a type I error is merely reported (e.g. $p = 0.053$), allowing the reader to make their own interpretation.

Type II errors, or beta (β) errors, often get overlooked as a result of the preoccupation with type I errors. Type II errors relate to accepting the null hypothesis when the alternate hypothesis is actually correct. For a test of differences this corresponds to declaring that no difference exists between groups, when a difference does actually exist. Using the courtroom analogy, this would be like returning a verdict of innocence for a guilty individual. Committing a type II error might equate to dismissing as ineffective a treatment that could actually have an impact, or it may result in no further research being conducted into certain important areas, because it was wrongly concluded that they were dead ends. In areas such as health and medicine, such an error could have serious negative ramifications.

There is an interrelationship between the chances of making a type I error and the chances of making a type II error. When the probability of making a type I error is low, the research is considered to be conservative. As the chance of committing a type I error rises, the research is considered to become more liberal. In terms of the courtroom, conservatism means that the jury tries to be as certain as possible that they do not convict an innocent person. Consequently, they are increasing the risk of letting a guilty person walk away free. So by setting a more demanding p value (e.g. less than 0.1 per cent, or $p < 0.001$), an investigator is increasing the chances of making a type II error. When a jury is liberal, their primary focus is ensuring that no guilty person is let off as innocent, which increases the chances of accidentally convicting an innocent person. Similarly, having a less demanding p value (e.g. less than 10 per cent, or $p < 0.1$) means the probability of committing a type II error is reduced. A scientist must therefore consider which is the most important priority for their research. Is it more important to avoid a type I error or a type II error?

Statistical power

The probability of making a type II error is also reported as a percentage, but more typically investigators refer to statistical power. This term is the percentage chance of *not* making a type II error. So if the probability of making a type II error is 20 per cent, the statistical power would be 80 per cent (100% − 20% = 80%). We have already discussed the interrelation between type I errors and type II errors, so power will also be influenced by the p value. Ideally we would be able to minimise the risk of making a type I error, but maintain statistical power as high as possible. One way in which statistical power can be raised without altering the p value is through increasing the number of subjects in each sample. By increasing the size of the sample, the estimates made about the population parameters, based upon sample statistics, become more accurate. The larger the sample, the less likely it is that its mean will deviate substantially from the mean of the population. The mean amount of physical activity performed by a sample of 10,000 adult females is less likely to deviate from the mean for the population of adult females than the mean of a sample of 10 adult females. The reduced error, referred to as the standard error of the mean, makes it likely that the means of two much larger samples drawn from the same population will differ by less than two smaller samples. The standard error of the difference is therefore generally lower for larger samples than for smaller samples with the same variance. As a result, a researcher can be more confident that the means of two samples are, or are not, different from each other. This equates to a reduction in type I error, concomitant with an increase in statistical power. This is one of the reasons why most experiments seek to achieve the maximum possible number of subjects in each sample.

One-tailed and two-tailed tests of difference

The example above details a two-tailed test of difference. In these circumstances the investigator is looking to detect a difference between the sample means. They do not make a prejudgement about whether the first sample will be higher or lower than the second sample.

A one-tailed test of difference relates to an alternate hypothesis that states the *direction* of difference. By direction, we mean whether one sample will be higher or lower than another. Examples of alternate hypotheses appropriate for one-tailed testing are listed below:

H_a State anxiety will be higher in female rugby players before competition than before training.
H_a Endurance runners will have lower body fat percentages than power athletes.
H_a The angular velocity of the club head at the moment of ball contact will be greater in golfers with a sub 4 handicap, when compared to golfers with a handicap greater than 16.

These types of hypotheses can only be used when there is already strong evidence in existence that indicates that a difference does lie in a particular direction (either higher or lower). In these instances the researcher's aim focuses on the size of the difference. The advantage of a one-tailed approach, in these cases, is that the full 5 per cent of the area representing the type I error is placed at the appropriate end of the distribution curve (Figure 5.4). This allows the researcher to declare a significant difference between samples, with a smaller actual difference between the recorded means.

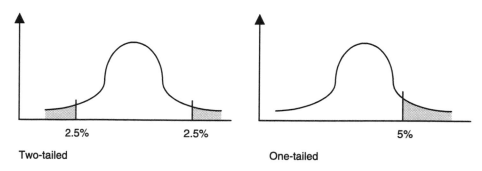

| 2.5% | 2.5% | 5% |

Two-tailed   One-tailed

Figure 5.4 One- and two-tailed tests of difference

One-tailed testing also leads to greater statistical power because a greater probability of declaring a significant difference means less chance of *not* declaring a significant difference, and accepting the null hypothesis (correctly or incorrectly).

Measuring differences between independent samples

The term independent samples refers to samples where the members of one sample are different and unrelated to the members of another sample. The tests used to measure difference in independent samples are subtly different from those used to test for difference in dependent samples.

Independent samples t tests

An independent samples t test is used to measure difference between the means of two samples comprising different people. The basic formula for a t test is given in Equation 5.2.

Equation 5.2

$$t = \frac{\bar{X}_1 - \bar{X}_2}{SE_D}$$

$\bar{X}_1$ = mean of sample one
$\bar{X}_2$ = mean of sample two
SE_D = standard error of the difference

Remember that the standard error of the difference is an estimate of the standard deviation for the population of chance differences. A t test is therefore merely a ratio of the actual difference between the means of the two samples $(\overline{X}_1 - \overline{X}_2)$ against the average difference expected by chance alone. Using the knowledge you have gained thus far, have a guess at how many times bigger the difference between the means must be $(\overline{X}_1 - \overline{X}_2)$ than the standard error of the difference for you to be 95 per cent certain that the difference between samples is not a chance difference (i.e. $p < 0.05$).

If you guessed approximately two times greater, you are correct. Recall that 95.44 per cent of the population of chance differences lie within two standard error of the differences either side of the mean, which was zero (Figure 5.3). If the measured difference between the means is twice as big as the standard error of the difference (giving a t score of 2), then you can be 95.44 per cent certain that this is not merely a chance difference. To be exactly 95 per cent certain, the t score needs to be reduced slightly to 1.96 (in other words the measured difference is 1.96 times as large as the standard error of the difference). Theoretically, a researcher would normally be looking for a t score of greater than 1.96 to declare a significant difference between samples. However, there is one final complication that needs to be taken into account. When we perform a t test, we make an estimate of the standard error of the difference, based upon the variance within each sample. This estimate under-predicts the true size of the standard error of the difference when it is based on data from a sample. The smaller the sample, the greater the extent of the under-prediction. This leads to the t score being inflated (because the denominator of the equation is reduced). This phenomenon was first described by William Sealey Gossett (1876–1937). Gossett wrote under the pseudonym of Student. Gossett or Student calculated how to adjust for this inflation, depending on how many cases, or pieces of data, are in each sample. Consequently, in a smaller sample we require a larger t score to arise for statistical significance to be declared than for a larger sample. Hence, a t test where the adjustment is made for the number of subjects, or cases, is referred to as a Studentised t test.

The t score required to produce a p value that is significant depends upon the sample size. At the $p < 0.05$ level (where we are at least 95 per cent certain we are not making a type I error), the t score needed will range from ~2.4 in small samples to 1.96 in much larger samples. In very small samples ($n < 5$), the t score required for significance will be higher than this range; generally t tests are not performed on samples of this size. Chapter 9 contains a more detailed discussion of interpreting p values.

Assumptions for an independent samples t test

Most statistical tests have various laws to which the data being analysed must adhere. These laws are called assumptions, and when they are broken it is termed 'violating the assumptions'. When the assumptions of a statistical test are violated, the results of the test may become invalid. For this reason we ensure the assumptions are not violated. The assumptions for a dependent samples t test are as follows:

- The data must be normally distributed, being drawn from a population where the scores are normally distributed. Otherwise the relationships between variance and the predictable spread of scores on which the test is founded will not hold true.
- Samples must be randomly selected from their populations. If this is not the case, then the principle of statistical inference (making predictions about the population based upon sample data) cannot be met.

- The variance of each sample must be approximately equal, which is known as homogeneity of variance. If the standard deviation of one sample is more than twice as large as for the other sample, then this is an indication that this assumption may be violated.

Dependent samples (repeated measures/paired samples) t tests

Dependent samples are samples that are related to one another. Often they contain the same people being measured on different occasions, hence statistical tests designed for use on dependent samples may be called repeated measures. A repeated measures t test may be used to test golfers for differences in the accuracy of a putting task, before and after a psychological intervention such as visualisation. In this example the same subjects would be measured on two occasions. The first measurement would be taken before the visualisation strategy was taught to, and implemented by, the subjects. The second measurement would be taken after the subjects had performed the visualisation strategy.

The repeated measures t test is attempting to detect differences between the two sets of scores. Theoretically, even though the subjects remain the same people, the two scores are considered to be different samples drawn from different populations. The first sample is drawn from a population of golfers who have not used visualisation. The second sample comes from a population of golfers who have used visualisation. The test will look at their accuracy scores for the putting tasks on the two different testing occasions and see whether a significant difference exists. The great advantage of the repeated measures design is that it is the same people who are being measured in both instances. The only change between the two samples is therefore assumed to be the psychological intervention. Of course, other factors may alter between testing sessions, but the extra chance difference between the means of the samples that may arise from the samples comprising different people is removed. This helps to remove all the extraneous variables associated with differences between individuals (e.g. height, intelligence, skill level, age etc.) and enables us to view the treatment effect more clearly.

When there is a relationship between samples, it means that the two samples are correlated. This will be discussed in greater depth in the next chapter, but it is necessary to have a rudimentary understanding of the concept to appreciate what is involved in repeated measures t tests. Correlated samples mean that a score in one sample is related to the paired score in the other sample. In repeated measures, the paired scores relate to the two scores measured for the same subject on the two testing occasions, e.g. one before the treatment and one after the treatment. These two scores are related in that an individual getting a relatively high score prior to the treatment will still get a high score after the treatment. Similarly, someone getting a relatively low score before a treatment will still get a low score following the treatment. The most accurate putter in a group may improve their putting following visualisation, but they will still be the best putter (or one of the best) following the visualisation. An inaccurate putter may also improve their score, but they will still be around the bottom of the group for putting accuracy because everybody may have improved slightly. There could be some changing within the group, as some people react more to the visualisation than others, and so creep above them in the rankings. However, generally individuals within the group will maintain their position in terms of putting accuracy. The less movement there is of

69

individuals' relative scores and positions within the group, the stronger the correlation between the scores before (sample 1) and after the treatment (sample 2).

It is not only repeated measures samples that have strong correlations in this way. Sometimes researchers use matched samples. The usual ways in which matched samples operate is that one large sample is selected. The two subjects with the highest score on the dependent variable are then randomly assigned to sample 1 or sample 2. Then the next two highest samples are randomly assigned in the same way. This continues until all members of the large sample are either part of sample 1 or sample 2. One of these samples is then given some intervention and the other is not. They are measured following this process, to investigate differences between the treated group and the non-treated group. These two groups are then regarded as two dependent samples. The scores will be related in the same way as repeated measures, because the first subject in sample 1 will have a high score, as will the first subject in sample 2. In the same way, the last subjects in both samples will have low scores. For this reason a dependent samples t test is also used on matched samples.

A dependent samples t test uses the same basic formula as an independent samples t test (Equation 5.3).

Equation 5.3

$$t = \frac{\bar{X}_1 - \bar{X}_2}{SE_D}$$

The difference between the two techniques is that the standard error of the difference is calculated in a different way for a dependent samples t test. In this form of the test, the standard error of the difference is adjusted to take into account the strength of the correlation between the two samples. Related samples have a lower probability of differing from one another by chance alone. The dependent samples t test produces a smaller standard error of the difference, which is adjusted to the value of the correlation. As a result, smaller mean differences may be calculated to be significantly different between dependent samples than with independent samples.

Assumptions for a dependent samples t test

- All the assumptions for the dependent samples t test apply to a dependent samples t test.
- The samples must be related, therefore it is important that you understand when to use which type of t test.

SPSS guidance for independent and dependent samples t tests

Instructions for performing t test analysis on SPSS is covered in detail in Chapter 6 of Coakes and Stead (2001).

Testing differences between more than two samples

So far we have dealt with the t test, which is a technique for examining two samples. As researchers, we may have more than two samples that we wish to test for difference.

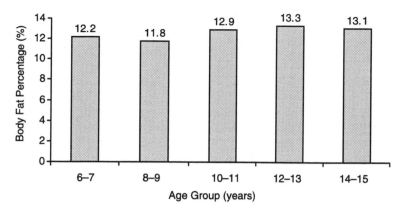

Figure 5.5 Differences in body fat percentage for children of different ages

Consider a study where a researcher is looking at differences in anthropometric data between five different age groups (Figure 5.5). When we are dealing with measuring differences between two samples (A and B), we only have to make one comparison, between A and B. When we have three samples (A, B and C), then we have to make three comparisons, between A versus B, A versus C, and B versus C. If we introduce an extra group, how many comparisons do we now have to make?

That's right, it is six comparisons (A versus B, A versus C, A versus D, B versus C, B versus D and C versus D). Table 5.1 shows the continuation of this pattern. The pattern shows us how many comparisons we would have to make to ensure every sample had been tested for difference against every other sample. It can be thought of as the number of games that would need to be played if every sample were a football team, and you wanted to ensure that every team had played each other once. The point of this is that as we increase the number of samples we want to examine, we have to keep making more and more comparisons. If we had six samples, we would have to perform 15 separate t tests which would be inconvenient, but there would also be another problem.

This problem is known as familywise error. When we perform one t test and use a

Table 5.1 Pattern for multiple comparisons

Number of samples	Number of comparisons
1	0
2	1
3	3
4	6
5	10
6	15
7	21
8	28
9	36
10	45

threshold of $p < 0.05$, we are saying there is a 5 per cent chance, or a one in twenty chance, of making a type I error (incorrectly accepting the alternate hypothesis). Now if we continue to perform t tests on the same set of data, each time using a value of $p < 0.05$, overall we are increasing our chance of making a type I error. It is a bit like buying additional tickets for a lottery – sooner or later you are going to win yourself the prize, or make a type I error.

There is a method to calculate familywise error and make adjustments to the p value based upon the extent of familywise error. However, using multiple t tests is a convoluted route to testing for difference in more than two samples. An alternative technique was developed by the statistician Ronald Aylmer Fisher (1890–1962) called analysis of variance (ANOVA). ANOVA analyses all the mean differences simultaneously and is therefore not susceptible to familywise error. ANOVA is an extremely commonly used technique in the field of sport and exercise science. Rather than generate a t score, ANOVA results in an *F* score (named after Fisher).

Simple one-way analysis of variance (ANOVA)

Just like t tests, ANOVA can be used for independent samples or dependent samples. In the instance of examining differences in a given dependent variable between different populations (independent samples), we use a simple one-way ANOVA. It essentially aims to achieve the same outcome as a t test, which is to compare the difference between the means of a number of samples to see whether they are larger than the differences expected by chance alone.

The basic formula for ANOVA is shown in Equation 5.4.

Equation 5.4

$$F = \frac{MS_B}{MS_E}$$

MS_B = mean square between MS_E = mean square error

In this formula the mean square between represents the amount that each sample mean differs from the average score. It gives us a measure of how much the means for each sample differ from one another. The mean square error is similar to the standard error of the difference, in that it provides an estimate of how much the means of samples randomly drawn from the same population might be expected to differ by chance alone. Hence, the *F* score is a ratio comparing the actual measured mean differences against the chance difference. Interpreting the size of the *F* score depends on the number of samples and the number of subjects within each the samples. Again, the *F* score is associated with a p value, the lower the p value, the less chance of making a type I error.

Assumptions for a simple one-way ANOVA

The assumptions for a one-way analysis of variance are the same as the assumptions for an independent samples t test. These are:

• random sample selection

- normality of data
- homogeneity of variance.

SPSS guidance for simple one-way ANOVA

Chapter 7 in Coakes and Steed (2001) covers one-way analysis of variance.

One-way repeated measures analysis of variance (ANOVA)

A researcher may wish to conduct an ANOVA on three or more dependent samples, in the same way as a repeated measures t test is used to detect difference between two dependent samples. The aim is again to remove the extra chance difference between the means of the samples arising from the samples comprising different people. With three or more samples, however, the additional samples might arise from more than one intervention being applied (e.g. golfers exposed to no treatment, visualisation, thought stopping, and mental relaxation techniques), or different dosages of a treatment (e.g. golfers exposed to no treatment, 5 minutes of visualisation, 10 minutes of visualisation, and 30 minutes of visualisation).

Assumptions for a one-way repeated measures ANOVA

- All the assumptions for a simple one-way ANOVA apply to a repeated measures ANOVA.
- The samples must be related.
- The relationships between each sample must be of approximately similar strength; this is known as homogeneity of covariance and, together with homogeneity of variance, relates to the assumption of sphericity. In other words, the strength of the correlation between sample 1 and sample 2 must be similar in strength to the correlation between sample 2 and sample 3, and between sample 1 and sample 3. One quick method of determining whether the assumption of sphericity has been violated or not is to check what is known as the Huynh-Feldt epsilon value (provided in the SPSS output). If this value is greater than 0.75, the assumption has not been substantially violated, whereas if it is less than this value, then the Huynh-Feldt adjusted values should be referred to (see Chapter 10 of Coakes and Steed 2001).

SPSS guidance for one-way repeated measures ANOVA

Chapter 10 in Coakes and Steed (2001) refers to the procedures for carrying out a one-way repeated measures ANOVA using SPSS.

Post hoc testing

A significant F score for an ANOVA will tell you that a significant difference exists between some of the samples. It could be that all samples are different from all others, or that only two samples differ from each other. The way to discover where the differences lie is to use a post hoc test. Post hoc means 'after the fact'. It is a term that covers a number of tests that can be carried out to establish which specific samples are significantly different from one another, after the ANOVA has been conducted. Typically a post hoc test will provide something called an interval size. The interval size is a value that corresponds to the unit in which the dependent variable is measured. For body fat, the interval size could be given as a percentage; for golf putting accuracy it would be given in cm. The interval size is a value that is the amount by which the means of two samples must differ in order to be significantly different from each other. For the example we used earlier, looking at the body fat percentage of five different age groups (Figure 5.5), if the interval size were 1.2 per cent, any samples whose mean differs by more than 1.2 per cent body fat are considered to be significantly different from one another. Figure 5.6 highlights the means which differ from each other by more than this amount, representing significant differences. From Figure 5.6, we can see that the only significant differences lie between the 8–9 year olds and two other groups, the 12–13s and 14–15s. Only these differences are greater than the interval size of 1.2 per cent.

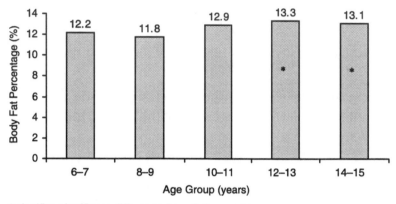

* signifies significant difference from 8–9 year olds

Figure 5.6 Post hoc analysis for body fat percentage of different ages

The level of significance (p value) that the investigator will accept must be decided prior to conducting a post hoc analysis. The level of significance (usually 0.05, 0.01 or 0.001) will affect the value of the interval size that is calculated in the analysis. A smaller significance level (e.g. 0.001) represents a smaller probability of committing a type I error, and will therefore produce a larger interval size.

As previously mentioned, there are different post hoc tests available to statisticians. Some will be more conservative, meaning the probability of committing a type I error is kept low. Others are more liberal, meaning that the risk of a type I error is larger, but the test has more statistical power. The two most commonly used post hoc tests are the Scheffé test, which is the most conservative, and the Tukey test, which is more liberal. You should understand what your priority is when selecting a post hoc test. Choose a more conservative test if your priority is avoiding a type I error, or choose a more liberal one to reduce the risk of a type II error.

Factorial analysis of variance

In our previous examples for tests of difference, there has been a single independent variable which defines the samples for independent samples (e.g. age group), or dependent samples (e.g. with or without the use of visualisation). This independent variable differentiates the samples; we hypothesise that the dependent variable (e.g. body fat percentage, or putting accuracy) will depend upon the independent variable. For instance, body fat percentage would depend upon age group, therefore the alternate hypothesis would expect to detect differences in different age groups (independent variable) for body fat percentage (dependent variable). In analysis of variance the independent variable is called a factor.

In some experimental designs a researcher might be interested in having more than one factor. Looking at changes in body fat percentage for different age groups is interesting, but what about gender differences at various ages? It might be more informative to look at samples of boys and girls at different age groups to see if a gender difference for body fat percentage becomes particularly pronounced at any age group. In this design there are two factors: age and gender. A test of difference would be looking for differences in gender and differences in age group simultaneously. This is the reason it is referred to as a two-way ANOVA, because in the two-dimensional representation of this type of design (Figure 5.7), analysis is conducted in two directions, vertically for gender, and horizontally for age group. The interaction effect would determine whether there was a gender difference present at a particular age group, but not at others.

It is possible to introduce additional factors, for example if you brought in activity levels (low, medium or high) in addition to age group and gender. However, it should be noted that multifactorial designs of this nature can start to become convoluted and difficult to recruit enough subjects for, if too many factors are used. How many subjects overall would be required in order to have 10 subjects in each sample for an experiment involving five age groups, two genders and three activity levels? The answer is 300 subjects ($10 \times 5 \times 2 \times 3$).

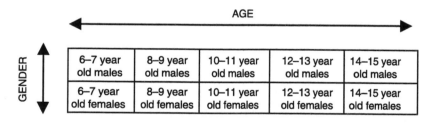

Figure 5.7 Schematic of a two-way design

Common mistakes

1 Performing multiple t tests without making a correction for familywise error.
2 Using difference tests for independent samples, when in fact the samples are dependent (repeated measures).
3 Attempting to examine every independent variable simultaneously, using an overly complicated factorial ANOVA, when there are too few subjects for this type of analysis.
4 Focusing purely on the statistical significance of a difference (p value) rather than the actual value of any difference between means (see Chapter 9).

SUMMARY

Difference testing is probably the most common form of statistical test used in sport and exercise science. Difference tests are usually employed on data derived from a longitudinal design, a true experimental design, or a quasi-experimental design (see Chapter 3). The tests seek to establish whether a difference lies between two or more groups.

The key factors to think about when selecting the appropriate test are:

- the number of groups or samples;
- whether they are independent or dependent samples;
- the number of factors.

Table 5.2 gives guidance on how to select the appropriate test.

Table 5.2 Selecting the right test of difference

	Statistical test			
	Independent samples *t* test	Dependent samples *t* test	One-way ANOVA	One-way rm* ANOVA
Only two samples	✓	✓	✗	✗
Independent samples	✓	✗	✓	✗
Dependent samples	✗	✓	✗	✓
More than one factor	✗	✗	✗	✗

* repeated measures

6

TESTS OF RELATIONSHIP

All mathematical laws which we find in Nature are always suspect to
me, in spite of their beauty. They give me no pleasure. They are merely
auxiliaries. At close range it is all not true.

Georg Christoph Lichtenberg (1959)

LEARNING OUTCOMES

Following this chapter you should be able to:

1   comprehend the concept of different types of relationships between variables;
2   identify the appropriate situation for the use of multiple regression and select the
     correct form of multiple regression to match your research question;
3   interpret the results of a range of statistical tests of relationship.

Prior to this section you should be familiar with the following terms:

* variables
* X and Y axes
* standard deviation.

Introduction

Relationships are important to sport and exercise science. Statistically a relationship
refers to the association between two sets of scores. This might be between two different
variables, such as height and weight, or it might be between two sets of scores, as it was
when we examined dependent samples in the previous chapter (see p. 62).

Below is a list of pairs of variables. Imagine the same individuals were measured on
the pair of variables and, based upon your knowledge, think which pairs you would
expect be related to each other.

* *height* and *body mass*
* *state anxiety* and *10,000-metre running performance*
* *peak power output in a Wingate test* and *100-metre sprint time*
* *club head velocity at ball strike* and *golf shot distance*
* *vertical jump height* and *1500-metre swim time*
* *measure of self-efficacy* and *score on a netball shooting task*
* *cross-sectional area of a muscle* and *the force exerted by that muscle*
* *ground reaction force during running* and *elbow joint range of motion during running*
* *percentage body fat* and *distance covered running for 12 minutes.*

You probably felt that some of these pairs would definitely be related, were you to measure individuals on both variables. Other pairs of variables you might have felt would not have been related closely. You may have considered that some variables were related, but that they would not be as strongly related as other pairs of variables. Take height and body mass for example. Is it the case that the taller you are, the greater your mass is? Height represents just a single dimension in body size – breadth and depth must also be considered; in other words, the body volume. You can probably picture a short, stocky person who would weigh more than a taller but leaner individual. Body density and composition, as well as body volume, will also influence the body mass of an individual. However, most people with a height of 180 cm will have a greater mass than people with a height of 150 cm. We can see, then, that there is some relationship between these variables, but it is not a perfect relationship.

In other examples the relationship may be stronger: take the cross-sectional area of a muscle and the force exerted by the muscle during a voluntary contraction. Although there are neurological factors connected with the specific tension of the muscle, which will influence the force exerted by a muscle, most of what affects the force exerted can be explained by the size of the muscle (which we can estimate based upon its cross-sectional area). In this instance the strength of the relationship, while still not perfect, is likely to be stronger than that found between height and body mass. In order to assess the importance of a relationship, an investigator needs some technique to assess its strength.

Scatter plots

A scatter plot is a common type of graph that allows us to simply evaluate the strength of a relationship between two variables. The X axis represents values on one variable (usually the one viewed as the independent variable) and the Y axis represents values for the other variable (usually the dependent variable). If we take height and body mass, we might place height on the X axis and body mass on the Y axis (Figure 6.1), because in this case we are evaluating to what extent body mass is dependent upon height. The marked point on the graph represents an individual with a height of 183 cm and a body mass of 70 kg. It is important to remember that in this type of graph, each point

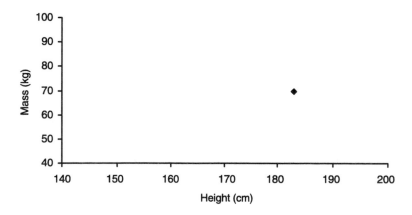

Figure 6.1 Height versus body mass

represents an individual subject. The individual's two scores for each variable (e.g. height and body mass) provide a co-ordinate which locates them on the two-dimensional space of the graph, each dimension being formed by one of the axes.

Figure 6.2 shows what happens when we add in a number of data points, each of which corresponds to a different subject. This type of graph is referred to as a scatter plot, because of the scatter of data points which it produces.

From this we can see that the scatter broadly forms an ellipse which is inclined so that it rises diagonally upwards from the origin of the graph. The two crucial factors to this scatter plot are its incline and the width of the ellipse. The incline tells us that the lower a subject's value for height, the lower their value for body mass is likely to be, or that the higher a subject's value for height, the higher their mass is likely to be (Figure 6.2). This provides one indication of the existence of a relationship between two variables.

The significance of the width of the ellipse becomes apparent when you look at two different scatter plots with different width ellipses. Figure 6.3 presents the scatter plots for different pairs of variables. You will notice a wider ellipse for the height versus body mass data than for the muscle cross-sectional area versus force data. A wide ellipse is representative of a large amount of variance on one variable, for a given value on another variable. Looking at Figure 6.3, you can see that if we use the ellipse to give an indication of how the two variables relate to each other, a height of 170 cm is associated with a range of values for body mass (55–91 kg). This means that a single value of the X variable (e.g. a height of 170 cm) corresponds to a range of values for the Y variable (e.g. a body mass of 55–91 kg). When we select a single value on the X variable, we are removing any variance from this variable. Therefore, the variance that we see in the Y variable, shown by the range of values, cannot be a result of variance in the X variable. The two variables can be said to vary independently. The less the variables vary independently, the stronger the relationship between variables is considered to be. In examining the scatter plot for muscle cross-sectional area versus force, we can see that for a single value on the X variable (cross-sectional area of 50 cm^2), the range of values on the Y variable associated with this value is quite small (force of 220–310 N). A smaller amount of independent variance is indicative of two variables that are more strongly related.

The less independent variance that exists, the more the variables can be seen to vary

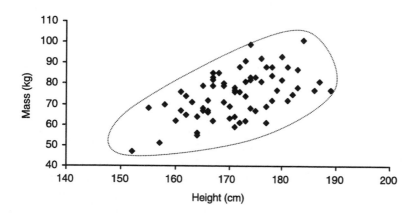

Figure 6.2 Scatter plot of height versus body mass

(a) Height versus Mass

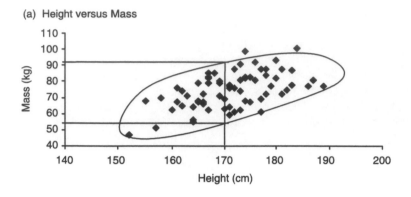

(b) CSA versus Force

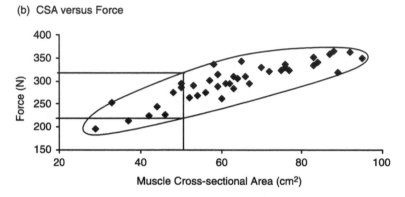

Figure 6.3 Relationships of different pairs of variables

together around the means of the group. The values on both variables move above and below the mean coincidentally. This is called common variance. When the relationship is strong (with a narrow ellipse), it might be that a score that is one standard deviation above the mean on variable X might correspond to a score of between 0.9 and 1.1 standard deviations above the mean for variable Y. A weaker relationship (with a wide ellipse) might see a score that is one standard deviation above the mean for variable Y correspond to a score of between 0.2 and 1.8 standard deviations above the mean. The same type of pattern would be seen for values below the mean. With a perfect relationship, a score that is one standard deviation above the mean on variable X would correspond to a value that is exactly one standard deviation above the mean in variable Y. Similarly, a score of 0.5 standard deviations below the mean on variable X would correspond to a score of 0.5 standard deviations below the mean for variable Y. How would the scatter plot look for a perfect relationship?

The answer is that it would form a straight line (Figure 6.4). With biological variables, it is unlikely that you will find the presence of a perfect relationship, as the interaction between numerous different factors is usually too complex to allow two variables to be perfectly related. However, some of the data you come across in biomechanics might form perfect, or near perfect, relationships (depending on the measurement error), such as looking at the relationship between impulse and height jumped in a standing vertical jump.

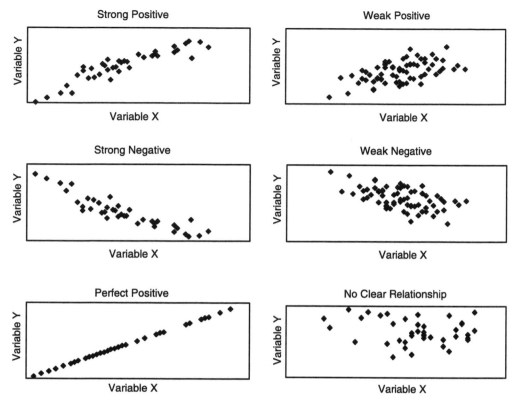

Figure 6.4 Patterns in scatter plots

It is also possible that you might find what is referred to as a negative relationship. This is one where the higher the value on the X variable, the lower the value is for the Y variable, and vice versa. A common example of this is where running time is one of the variables. Take the example of peak power in a Wingate test versus 100-metre sprint time. We would expect the subjects producing high amounts of power to be quicker over 100 metres, which would mean the time taken to complete 100 metres would be low. Similarly, subjects producing low amounts of power may be more likely to take longer to complete 100 metres, thus their 100-metre times would be high. In this case the negative relationship is really only an artefact of the way in which we have measured sprint speed. Were we to use average running velocity over 100 metres instead, the relationship would become a positive relationship reflecting the true relationship that we would instinctively expect between peak power output and sprint speed. However, there are some variables which would have a true negative relationship, in the sense that if you have high values for one variable, you would expect to see low values in the other. Think about the $\dot{V}O_2$ max of individuals and their heart rate when cycling at 150 W. You might expect to see those individuals with a higher $\dot{V}O_2$ max tending towards having a lower HR during the exercise. Those with lower $\dot{V}O_2$ max may tend to have higher HR values whilst cycling at 200 W.

Scatter plots enable a researcher to begin to understand relationships between variables and should act as the first step of investigating any relationships between variables. Figure 6.4 shows the types of pattern that you should try to look for. This first stage of looking at graphical representations of data is often termed 'eyeballing' the data.

Correlations

Although scatter plots give an indication of relationships, it is difficult to assess the relative strengths of different relationships by sight alone. Also, to produce an effective scatter plot, at least 20 data points are required, which means having at least 20 subjects from which to collect data. There is a statistical technique called correlation, which allows a researcher to quantify the strength of the relationship between two variables. The most commonly used form of correlation is one known as Pearson's product moment correlation coefficient, which was devised by the English statistician Karl Pearson (1857–1936). The correlation coefficient provides a value between −1 and +1. A value of −1 denotes a perfect negative relationship, while a value of +1 signifies a perfect positive relationship, and a value of 0 indicates the complete absence of any relationship between the two variables. The correlation coefficient can of course take any intermediate value between −1 and +1. For example, a value of +0.9 would denote a strong positive relationship, whereas +0.4 would represent only a very weak relationship.

The formula for Pearson's product moment correlation coefficient is shown by Equation 6.1.

Equation 6.1

$$r = \frac{\Sigma(Z_X Z_Y)}{N}$$

Σ = sum of
Z_X = Z scores for X
Z_Y = Z scores for Y
N = number of subjects/cases

In order to appreciate how this equation works, it is necessary to understand what a Z score is. A Z score converts each raw score into a value that tells us how many standard deviations a score is away from the mean value. If the mean height of a group were 170 cm and the standard deviation for the group were 10 cm, an individual who was 180 cm would have a Z score of +1 (i.e. one standard deviation higher than the mean). If their height had been 160 cm, their Z score would be −1 (i.e. one standard deviation below the mean). The Z score for an individual who was 176 cm would therefore be . . .?

Answer: +0.6 or 0.6 of a standard deviation above the mean.

Having converted each individual's raw score to a Z score for both the X variable and the Y variable, these scores are then multiplied together. When this has been done for each individual in the group, all these values are added together to give $\Sigma(Z_X Z_Y)$. In the case of two variables that are strongly positively related, the Z scores for both variables should be closely matched. Those individuals with a high positive Z score for variable X should have a high positive Z score for variable Y, and those with a high negative Z score for variable X should have the same for variable Y. When these Z scores are multiplied together, those that match up in terms of sign (+ or −) will result in a positive value. If you multiply a positive Z score by another positive Z score, you will obtain a positive value; similarly if you multiply a negative Z score by a negative Z score, you will also get a positive value.

Negative values arise when the signs do not match up and you get a positive Z score being multiplied by a negative Z score. When a large number of the scores on both variables match up to produce positive products, the correlation coefficient will be a high positive number. When the reverse is true and there is a trend of most signs not matching, the correlation coefficient will be a high negative number. When there is no pattern present, with some signs matching and some not matching, the products will be a mixture of positive and negative values. When these are summed to calculate $\Sigma(Z_X Z_Y)$, sometimes you will be adding numbers, sometimes subtracting; this will lead the correlation coefficient to be a low number (whether slightly positive or slightly negative).

It is possible then to use the correlation coefficient score (known as the r score) to give an indication of the strength of the relationship, as well as the type of relationship (positive or negative). Just as with tests of difference, however, correlations are subject to occurrence by chance alone. Imagine having two bags full of random numbers. First you draw five numbers out of bag number one; the first number drawn is allocated to subject one, the second number to subject two, etc. Now you do the same for bag two, drawing another five numbers and allocating them to the same subjects. It is not inconceivable that the first subject receives two low numbers from the two bags. The second subject may possibly receive two high numbers. Should the remaining three subjects receive a selection of numbers interspersed between the first two pairs of numbers, then the numbers drawn randomly from the two bags would be moderately positively correlated. So there is a possibility that a correlation can arise by chance alone. If this scenario were repeated thousands of times, sometimes there would be a moderate positive correlation, sometimes a moderate negative correlation, on other occasions there would be no correlation. More rarely a strong positive or negative correlation would emerge. With five subjects the probability of obtaining each different r score, by chance alone, is known. A correlation of $r = \pm 0.88$ for this many subjects would only have a 5 per cent probability of occurring by chance alone. This means that a correlation of a greater value would have a less than 5 per cent probability of occurring by chance alone. In this situation the alternate hypothesis states that a relationship does exist between two variables. Thus, for a correlation greater than ± 0.88 the probability of a type I error (incorrectly accepting the alternate hypothesis) would be less than 5 per cent ($p < 0.05$). The statistical significance of a correlation can be judged in much the same way as that of a test of difference, with a lower p value corresponding to greater statistical significance (see p. 115). As with tests of difference (see 'Type I and type II errors', p. 64), researchers will commonly use a threshold value (e.g. $p < 0.05$) to determine whether a correlation between two variables is significant or not, but it is becoming increasingly common to report the exact p value and allow the reader to interpret this.

Sample size and statistical significance

In the example referred to so far, only five subjects have been used. Clearly the probability of getting five sets of values to be related and produce a moderate correlation is greater than the probability of 100 sets of values to be correlated. The probability of the 100 numbers drawn out of bag one lining up against similar values drawn in the same order from bag two is much less likely. Therefore, the correlation associated with a $p < 0.05$ for 100 subjects, which means that an r score larger than this value would occur less than 5 per cent of the time by chance alone, is ± 0.20, as opposed to ± 0.88 for just 5 subjects. The p value of a correlation, representing its statistical significance, is influenced substantially by the number of cases, or subjects in a sample.

Size of a correlation coefficient

The p value will inform us of the probability of a type I error occurring, but this is not the same as the strength of the correlation. How closely the two variables are related is still signified by the r score, which relates to the extent of common variance seen between the two variables. We can quantify the amount of common variance (i.e. the extent to which the two variables vary together above and below their means) by squaring the r score (r^2). The r^2 value (also known as the coefficient of determination) is expressed as a percentage and tells us how much of the variance in one variable variance can be explained by variance in the other variable. The r^2 for a correlation of ± 0.9 informs us that 81 per cent ($0.9 \times 0.9 = 0.81 = 81\%$) of the variance in variable Y is accounted for by common variance with variable X. This leaves 19 per cent of the variance which is independent of variable X. An r score of ± 0.5 is not half the strength, but a quarter of the strength, of a correlation of ± 1.0, as the common variance accounts for only 25 per cent of the overall variance ($0.5 \times 0.5 = 0.25 = 25\%$).

Understanding correlations

Correlations quantify the relationship between two variables. Strong correlations are often interpreted as indicating the existence of a link between two variables, or even an influence of one variable on the other. The use of the terms 'dependent' and 'independent' variable reinforces this interpretation by supporting the concept that one variable is dependent upon another. However, it is in the interpretation of a correlation that the greatest potential for a misconception lies. When using correlation analysis you must be aware that a correlation in isolation can never be complete evidence that variance on one variable *causes* the variance in another. The discovery of a strong negative correlation between body fat percentage and distance covered in 12 minutes of running is not proof that low body fat percentage causes a runner to be able to cover more distance. It is no guarantee, even, that body fat percentage is responsible for distance covered. It would be tempting to conclude on the basis of the correlation that a lower body fat percentage would indicate that a greater percentage of body mass is comprised of lean muscle mass, which accounts for the better endurance performance. However, it may be a hidden association that these variables share with an underlying variable that might account for the relationship between these two variables, for example training volume. A high training volume might account for a low body fat percentage, as well as an improved endurance performance. That is not to say that reducing body fat percentage through dieting would necessarily improve 12 minute run performance. The interpretation of correlation is further discussed in Chapter 9 (see p. 117).

Bivariate regression

As well as allowing us to investigate and quantify the association between variables, a correlation also forms the first step in predicting an individual's score on one variable, based upon their score on another variable. It should be noted that it is only possible to predict with accuracy when there is a strong correlation between variables. A good example of this is using distance covered during 12 minutes of running to predict $\dot{V}O_2$ max. Because direct measurement of $\dot{V}O_2$ max is a time- and resource-intensive operation, scientists have searched for more convenient ways to obtain an indication. One proposed method has been to use distance covered during 12 minutes of running maximally to predict $\dot{V}O_2$ max, because of the relationship that has been found between these two variables.

The prediction is founded upon the line of best fit, which is a straight line that is drawn to minimise the distance between each individual data point and the straight line. The distance between each data point and the line of best fit is called a residual (Figure 6.5). The line of best fit is therefore designed to keep the residuals as small as possible. The value of all the residuals above the line is equal to the value of all the residuals below the line. The line therefore balances the points above the line with the points below.

The two important components of a line of best fit are the gradient, which describes the slope of the line, and the intercept, which informs us where the line intercepts the Y axis (Figure 6.5). These two components are calculated to produce the line of best fit, stating where it starts from and what route it follows. A negative gradient would be associated with a negative correlation. The variable that we use to predict is placed on the X axis, and is alternatively known as the predictor variable. Once we have constructed a line of best fit for the data, then we can use it to predict the score of an individual for whom we only have a score on the predictor variable (Figure 6.6). To do this a vertical line is drawn upwards corresponding to the value on the predictor

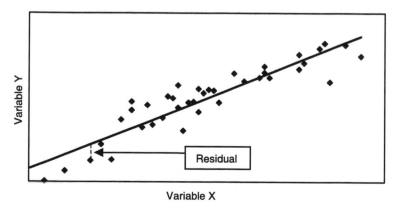

Figure 6.5 Line of best fit

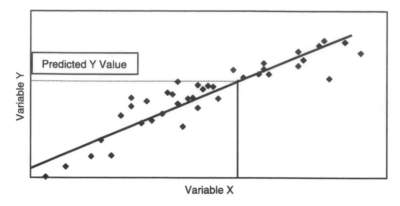

Figure 6.6 Predicting scores on one variable based upon scores on another

variable, which gives us the score on the other variable horizontally level with where it intercepts the line of best fit.

To obtain the predicted value for the Y variable mathematically, rather than using the graphical approach, Equation 6.2 is used.

Equation 6.2

$$Y = mX + C$$

Y = the value that is predicted for the Y variable
X = the raw score of the individual on the predictor variable
m = the gradient of the line of best fit
C = the Y intercept of the line of best fit

This equation is the standard equation for a straight line. Through multiplying the individual's actual score on the predictor variable by the gradient, we are effectively sliding along the line until we reach the correct X score. Through adding this value to the Y intercept, we are starting the line in the correct position.

The accuracy of the prediction is not perfect and to get an indication of the likely extent of the error involved in a prediction, we use the existing data that enabled us to calculate the line of best fit. We calculate something called the standard error of the estimate (SE_E). The SE_E works on the principle that any errors in future predictions using this line of best fit will follow the pattern of the data used to construct the line of best fit. Remember that each data point, representing a single subject, had a residual that measured the distance of that data point from the line of best fit (Figure 6.5). This residual is equivalent to the error for that data point in the prediction of Y, from the score on X (Figure 6.7). The standard error of the estimate is the average size of residual encountered in the data used to construct the line of best fit. The formula used to calculate the standard error of the estimate converts all the residuals to positive values, because you will recall that the residuals above the line (positive values) were equal to the residuals below the line (negative values). If this step were not taken, the average size of the residual would be zero. The SE_E thus gives us an indication of how much future predictions (or estimates) will err by on average. This value can be used

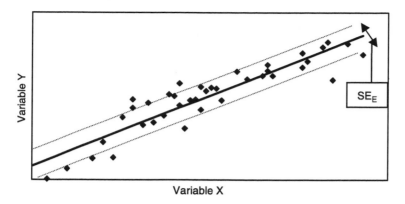

Figure 6.7 Standard error of the estimate

to represent the accuracy of predictions produced by regression (Figure 6.7). Weak correlations cannot be used for prediction purposes because the standard error of the estimate would be too high, meaning that the prediction would be too inaccurate to be of any use.

Assumptions for correlation and bivariate regression

- The data must be normally distributed for both variables.
- The residuals must be normally distributed, with the mean residual value being reflected by the standard error of the estimate and the residuals being normally distributed around this mean.
- The residuals should display a quality known as homoscedasticity. This is the quality of the residuals showing no bias towards values on the X variable. In other words, the residuals show no trend towards increasing towards either end of the range of values for the X variable. Figure 6.8 shows a scatter plot for data that do possess homoscedasticity, and data which do not. The latter example is called heteroscedasticity. Notice for this heteroscedastic data that as the X values get greater, the residuals also get greater. The pattern this produces has the appearance of a shot fired from a shotgun. The reverse situation also constitutes heteroscedasticity, where residuals get larger as the values of X decrease. This gives the appearance that the shotgun is being fired in the opposite direction.
- The relationship between the two variables must be linear, so that as one variable increases, so the other increases (or decreases in the case of a negative correlation) proportionately. Data may be related in a non-linear fashion; if this is the case then correlation and bivariate regression are inappropriate for quantifying and predicting from this type of relationship. Figure 6.9 demonstrates how the line of best fit will misrepresent the true trend of the data. The analysis of the nature of the type of relationship between variables is called trend analysis. There are numerous types of non-linear relationships, each of which can still be used to predict the values on one variable based upon another.

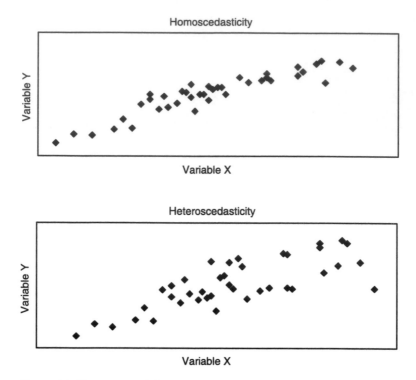

Figure 6.8 Homoscedasticity and Heteroscedasticity

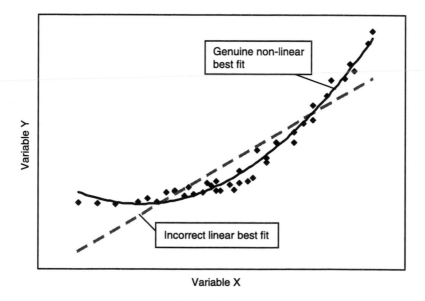

Figure 6.9 Non-linear relationships

Chapter 5 of Coakes and Steed (2001) covers correlation analysis.

Multiple regression

Bivariate regression involves the prediction of one variable based upon a single pre-dictor variable. Multiple regression incorporates the use of a number of predictor variables. Height was viewed as having a weak relationship with body mass (see p. 78) and would probably be little use in predicting body mass, but imagine if we could also use body fat percentage and an estimate of muscle mass in a combined predictive model.

Body mass is not particularly difficult to measure, so there would be little sense in going to all this trouble to predict body mass when we can measure it directly without any inconvenience. However, there are some variables that are very difficult to measure, or that we would like to know in advance, for which multiple regression is a useful tool. Say, for example, that we wished to know what distance a long jumper would obtain in the Olympic finals. There is little point in waiting until the Olympics and measuring how well they do, because by then it is too late to alter their performance. Also, we can't set up a replica of the Olympic finals to find out, as this is impractical. Instead, we could try to predict performance based upon some variables that we might be able to collect easily now, such as practice jump distance, psychological preparedness, leg power etc.

Multiple regression can also shed light on our understanding of the interactions between different variables. Whilst this approach cannot be taken in isolation as evi-dence that certain variables cause variance in another variable, it does help researchers get a better sense of which variables might contribute to variance on a particular variable, helping to direct further study.

Multiple regression gives us an R score, so that it can be differentiated from bivariate regression and the r score. The R^2 (also known as the coefficient of multiple determin-ation) tells us what percentage of the variance in the Y variable can be accounted for by variance in the X variables combined (X_1, X_2, ... X_N). There are three main types of multiple regression; each with a slightly different use and purpose. The first type is called standard multiple regression; this involves all the independent variables (X variables) that have been collected being put into the model simultaneously. This gives us the predictive power of all variables combined simultaneously.

The second type of analysis is called stepwise multiple regression; this places the independent variables into the equation one at a time. First, it begins with bivariate regression, where just one independent variable is used to predict the dependent vari-able. Then a second predictor variable is added to the model (so that two predictor variables are used), then the third predictor variable is added, and so on. At each stage the analysis provides an R^2 value to inform the researcher of the predictive power of the model at each stage. The variables are added into the model in an order that produces the best predictive model at each stage. So at the first step, the first predictor variable added into the model will always be the variable that has the strongest correlation with the dependent variable, because that will produce the best prediction. At the next step a predictor variable will be added in that produces the best prediction with two predictor variables. This is not necessarily the variable that has the next strongest correlation with the dependent variable. The reason why this is not the case is because of multicollinearity. Multicollinearity occurs when two or more of the predictor variables are strongly correlated amongst themselves. For instance, in trying to predict performance in 10,000-metre running, a researcher may use $\dot{V}O_2$ max, velocity at $\dot{V}O_2$ max, lactate threshold, running economy and body mass as predictor variables. The best predictor in a heterogeneous sample may be velocity at $\dot{V}O_2$ max, the next best predictor might be $\dot{V}O_2$ max. It does not follow that the best predictive model using two variables would be velocity at $\dot{V}O_2$ max and $\dot{V}O_2$ max. This is because these two variables would be strongly correlated with each other. By adding the two together, we would not be gaining much more of an explanation of what accounts for variance in 10,000-metre performance (the Y variable). The best model with two predictor variables may come instead from velocity at $\dot{V}O_2$ max and lactate threshold. On occasions two of the predictor variables will be perfectly correlated, exhibiting the property known as singularity. This usually occurs when one variable is a mathematical derivation of another variable. Stepwise multiple regression will continue to add additional variables into the model until the stage at which adding a further predictive variable does not significantly improve the predictive power of the model.

Hierarchical multiple regression is essentially the same as stepwise multiple regression except that rather than using statistical criteria to select the order of entry into the model, as with the stepwise procedure, the researcher dictates the order the predictor variables are entered into the model. The researcher usually has a rationale for the order (hierarchy) in which the variables are entered. This might be practical reasons, such as some variables being easier to measure than others, and so the researcher would rather use the variables that are easier to measure for predictive purpose. Alternatively, it might relate to theoretical reasons, such as previous research that has shown a particular relationship or interaction between the dependent variable and some predictor variables. Whichever type of multiple regression is selected, the investigator should be able to fully justify their selection of technique.

Assumptions for multiple regression

- Normal distribution of the raw scores and the residuals.
- Homoscedasticity of the residuals should be present.
- The relationship between predictor variables and the dependent variable should be linear.
- The ratio of cases, or subjects, to predictor variables should not be too low. Generally speaking there should be at least five subjects (although ideally 20 subjects should be used) for each predictor variable used in an analysis. In stepwise regression this ratio should be 40 subjects to each independent variable.

SPSS guidance for multiple regression

The procedures for performing multiple regression using SPSS is addressed in Chapter 17 of Coakes and Steed (2001).

Common mistakes

1 Evaluating the relative strength of a correlation based upon r, rather than r^2 (see p. 84).
2 Concluding that a strong correlation is evidence enough to demonstrate a causal link between two variables (see p. 84).
3 Focusing purely on the statistical significance of a correlation (p value) rather than the actual size of a correlation (r^2) (see Chapter 9).
4 Using bivariate regression to predict the score on the dependent variable when the standard error of the estimate (SE_E) is too large and leads to an inaccurate prediction.
5 Using multiple regression when there are too few subjects for the number of independent variables that are involved in the model.

SUMMARY

Correlation is extremely useful for determining the strength of a relationship between two variables. It is often used to assess the criterion validity (see Chapter 3) of a measurement technique, by measuring the association between a new technique and an established 'gold standard' measure of the same construct. Regression (bivariate or multiple) can be used to predict scores on a given dependent variable within a given range of data. However, when making predictions, a researcher must be careful not to extrapolate the line of best fit (which acts as the prediction line) beyond the range of the data which has been collected. This can result in an invalid prediction. The other major purpose of regression is to attempt to better understand the interactions between variables. Remember to be cautious in drawing conclusions about cause and effect purely based upon the predictive strength of a regression model.

7

NON-PARAMETRIC STATISTICS
AND MULTIVARIATE STATISTICS

> If your experiment needs statistics, you ought to have done a better
> experiment.
>
> Lord Ernest Rutherford

LEARNING OUTCOMES

Following this chapter you should be able to:

1 select the correct non-parametric test for the data you have collected;
2 interpret the results from a number of non-parametric statistical tests' difference
   and relationship.

Prior to this section you should be familiar with the following terms:

* normal and non-normal
* measurement scales
* p values.

Introduction

The statistical techniques that we have examined thus far are all parametric statistical
techniques. There are two situations in which non-parametric statistical techniques are
required. The first situation, as mentioned in Chapter 4, is when the data are not
normally distributed. The second set of circumstances, which often occurs in combination with the first situation, is when the data are measured on a scale that does not
involve equal units. This is contrary to most unit scales that we are used to dealing with.
For example, the interval between 1 kg and 2 kg is the same as the interval between
99 kg and 100 kg. This assumption cannot be made for other scales used within sport
and exercise science, particularly those based upon the subjective ratings of subjects.
The ratings of perceived exertion (RPE) scale is a good example of just such a scale. It
is difficult to know whether the interval between 6 and 7 on the scale is the same as the
interval between 19 and 20. It is also open to debate whether data collected using the
Likert scales to measure emotional state during sport should be analysed using parametric statistical techniques unless they have been validated as interval scales. Previous
research and experience have shown that such scales do often act as interval data, but
the question should always be asked whether or not parametric statistics are
appropriate for your data.

Ordinal scales

One of the techniques central to many non-parametric statistical tests is the conversion of the data to an ordinal scale. This involves giving each value a rank order as in Table 7.1.

In the conversion to an ordinal scale, the highest value is ascribed a value of 1, the next highest value becomes 2, and so on. The first effect of this conversion to an ordinal scale is to standardise distribution. The variance becomes standardised for the number of subjects there are. Take the two sets of skewed data in Table 7.2, one positively skewed and one negatively skewed, and the distribution becomes identical when we convert them to an ordinal scale. The other effect of using an ordinal scale is that it negates the problems of scales with unequal unit intervals. On an ordinal scale we are merely concerned with the rank order of the values, not by how much they differ from one another. With three scores valued 100, 5 and 1, it does not matter whether 100 is genuinely 20 times larger than 5, or 5 is exactly 4 equal units above 1. These scores are merely ranked 1 (100), 2 (5) and 3 (1).

Non-parametric statistical tests

The structure of parametric statistical testing is mirrored by non-parametric equivalents. So there are non-parametric tests of difference and non-parametric tests of relationship.

Table 7.1 Converting data to an ordinal scale

Original value (arbitrary units)	Ordinal scale
23	5
64	2
15	6
2	7
105	1
26	4
29	3

Table 7.2 Skewed data converted to an ordinal scale

Positively skewed (arbitrary units)	Ordinal scale	Negatively skewed (arbitrary units)	Ordinal scale
2	7	2	7
3	6	6	6
4	4	28	5
5	5	29	4
7	3	30	3
13	2	31	2
29	1	32	1

Tests of difference for independent samples

When the samples that are being tested for difference consist of different people whose scores are unrelated, there are two non-parametric statistical tests that are used. The first is the non-parametric equivalent of a t test and is therefore appropriate for testing difference between two samples. This test is named the Mann-Whitney U test. The other test is similar to a simple one-way analysis of variance and is suitable for three or more samples. This second test is known as a Kruskal-Wallis ANOVA. Both tests work on the same principles, involving rank ordering across samples.

Table 7.3 shows state anxiety prior to gymnastic competition for two age groups of male gymnasts (15 boys in each group). The scores have already been converted to an ordinal scale across both samples, the most anxious individual across both samples being scored as 1, the second most anxious as 2, etc. The researcher's hypothesis is that the older group of boys will have lower state anxiety than the younger boys prior to competition.

Note that tied scores on the original scale (e.g. two individuals both averaging 3.2 for state anxiety on the questionnaire scoring system) receive a fractional score (e.g. instead of being scored 4 and 5 on the ordinal scale, they both receive a score of 4.5). The principle behind both the Mann-Whitney U test and the Kruskal-Wallis ANOVA is that they compare the sum of the ranks (ΣR). This is the sum of all the scores in a sample when converted to an ordinal scale. In this situation the sample with the highest scores on the original scale will get a lower value for ΣR, because the highest score receives a 1 (the lowest number on an ordinal scale) and so on. Just as with parametric data, differences occur between samples drawn from the same population by chance alone. In our state anxiety example the scores ranged from 1–30. The sum of 1–30 is 465, having no difference between samples would mean that ΣR would be 232.5 for both samples. It is possible that two randomly drawn samples of 15 subjects would lead

Table 7.3 State anxiety for two different age groups of male gymnasts (scored on an ordinal scale)

	12–14 year olds	14–16 year olds
	1	4
	2	6
	3	8
	5	9
	7	13
	10	14
	11	16
	12	18
	15	19
	17	23
	20	25
	21	27
	22	28
	24	29
	26	30
ΣR	196	269

to an ΣR of 232.5 for both samples, but it more likely that there would be a slight difference between the samples.

The Mann-Whitney U test tells us whether the difference found between the ΣR for both samples is larger than that which we might reasonably expect to find by chance alone. The Kruskal-Wallis ANOVA performs the same function, except that it examines differences between the ΣR for three or more samples. Both tests produce a p value which represents the probability of committing a type I error (incorrectly accepting the alternate hypothesis, i.e. saying there is a difference between samples, when none exists). The p value can be assessed relative to any p value thresholds (e.g. $p < 0.05$) to determine the statistical significance of the difference.

Assumptions for the Mann-Whitney U test and the Kruskal-Wallis ANOVA

Non-parametric tests are generally considered to be more robust than their parametric equivalents, meaning that there are fewer assumptions that may potentially be violated. There is one assumption, however, that is relevant to all inferential statistical techniques; that is:

* The samples must be randomly selected. This is to ensure that they do not form a biased selection of the underlying population, about whom we make inferences based upon the sample statistics.

Tests of difference for dependent samples (repeated measures)

The Wilcoxon signed rank test is the non-parametric equivalent of a repeated measures t test. It allows a researcher to test for differences between two dependent samples. The test of difference for three or more dependent samples is called a Friedman test. Both tests operate in slightly different ways, but both involve conversion of data to an ordinal scale.

In calculating the Wilcoxon signed rank test, the differences between the two scores on the original scale for the same subject $(X_1 - X_2)$ are ranked for magnitude (Table 7.4). It is these rank scores that are then used in the calculation. Table 7.4 shows data for ratings of perceived exhaustion for 10 subjects during an aerobics class, before and after a 12-week aerobics training programme.

All those scores that produce a positive difference, where $X_1 > X_2$, are summed. This value (sum of positive ranks) is used to analyse whether the X_1 scores are significantly different from the X_2 scores. If all the X_1 scores had been higher than the X_2 scores, then all the ranks (1–10) would have been positive. The sum of positive ranks (SOPR) would have been 55 $(1 + 2 + 3 \ldots + 10)$. A value of 55 would indicate that X_1 scores are all higher than X_2, a pattern which is unlikely to occur by chance alone. If all the X_1 scores had been lower than the X_2 scores, then all the ranks (1–10) would have been negative. The SOPR would therefore have been zero. A value of zero would indicate that X_1 scores are all lower than X_2, a pattern which is again unlikely to occur by chance alone. For thousands of pairs of randomly drawn samples of 10 subjects, the average SOPR would be 27.5. From the thousands of randomly drawn pairs, we would expect some of the pairs to produce SOPR values greater than 27.5, and some pairs to produce SOPR values less than 27.5, but on average the value would be 27.5. The Wilcoxon signed rank test compares the actual SOPR from the two dependent samples, with the range of

Table 7.4 Ratings of perceived exhaustion during an aerobics class before and after training

Subject	RPE before training (X_1)	RPE after training (X_2)	$(X_1 - X_2)$	Rank
1	17	14	+3	5.5 (+)
2	14	13	+1	9.5 (+)
3	18	13	+5	2 (+)
4	13	14	−1	9.5 (−)
5	16	14	+2	7.5 (+)
6	12	8	+4	3.5 (+)
7	14	11	+3	5.5 (+)
8	17	11	+6	1 (+)
9	15	17	−2	7.5 (−)
10	18	14	+4	3.5 (+)
Sum of positive ranks				**38**

SOPR values that would be expected in 95 per cent of the cases where two samples are randomly drawn from the same sample. If the actual observed sum of positive ranks is outside of this range, then a significant difference is declared between the two samples.

The Friedman test uses a different method of ranking the scores across the dependent samples. Rather than rank the differences between the scores for the same individual on different testing occasions, the Friedman test ranks the raw scores for each subject relative to one another. Table 7.5 displays the data for an extension of the example we examined in Table 7.4. In this extension of the experiment, the subjects continued an additional 10 weeks of training, following the initial 10 weeks. Following this second period of training, the subjects underwent a third testing session, where RPE was measured during another aerobics session. You can see that for subject 1, RPE was highest before training, so this receives a 1, it was second highest after 10 weeks of training, so this receives a 2, the lowest value after 20 weeks receives a 3. This has been done for all the subjects. The ranks are summed for each of the three testing sessions (before training, after 10 weeks of training and after 20 weeks of training).

Table 7.5 Ratings of perceived exhaustion during an aerobics class before and after 10 and 20 weeks of training

Subject	RPE before training (X_1)	Rank (X_1)	RPE after 10 w training (X_2)	Rank (X_2)	RPE after 20 w training (X_3)	Rank (X_3)
1	17	1	14	2	13	3
2	14	1	13	2.5	13	2.5
3	18	1	13	2	11	3
4	13	2.5	14	1	13	2.5
5	16	1	14	3	15	2
6	12	1	8	3	10	2
7	14	1	11	3	12	2
8	17	1	11	2	10	3
9	15	3	17	1	16	2
10	18	1	14	2	13	3
	Rank total (X₁)	**13.5**	Rank total (X₂)	**21.5**	Rank total (X₃)	**25**

The rank totals are then compared for differences. Lower values for rank totals indicate that the raw scores on the original scale were high (because the highest scores receive low values on an ordinal scale, e.g. 1). Conversely, higher values for rank totals indicate that the raw scores on the original scale were low. The Friedman test compares the differences between these rank totals in comparison to the differences that might reasonably expected to occur by chance alone. As with all the tests of difference that we have examined, a p value is also produced for the Friedman test.

The samples for both the Wilcoxon signed rank test and the Friedman test should be randomly selected.

Relationship testing

The non-parametric test for measuring the strength of a relationship between two variables is called Spearman's rank order correlation coefficient. For this procedure the raw scores for both variables are converted to an ordinal scale. Once this has been done, the deviations are calculated. This is carried out by subtracting the score on the ordinal scale for variable X from the score on variable Y, for the same subject (Table 7.6). These deviations are then squared to convert them all into positive value, and then summed (Σd^2).

The sum of the deviations squared (Σd^2) will be low if the two variables are strongly positively related, because the values on the two variables should correspond, which would make the deviations small. This means 1 for variable X should line up with 1 for variable Y (or at least a number close in value to 1); the other values should follow the same pattern. When no relationship exists, the deviations will be larger, because the values for the two variables will not correspond, thus Σd^2 will be greater. When a strong negative relationship exists between the variables, then Σd^2 will be larger still. This is because in these circumstances the data should follow a pattern of creating maximum deviations. A value of 1 for variable X should correspond to a value of 10 for variable Y (or a number close to 10). The deviations will therefore tend towards being large, meaning that Σd^2 will also be large. The size of Σd^2 will also be affected by the number of subjects, because the more subjects there are, the more deviations that are calculated,

Table 7.6 Spearman's rank order correlation coefficient

Subject	Variable X (Ordinal scale)	Variable Y (Ordinal scale)	Deviations (X − Y)	Deviations squared (d^2)
1	4	3	+1	1
2	3	5	−2	4
3	6	6	0	0
4	9	10	−1	1
5	10	7	+3	9
6	1	1	0	0
7	2	2	0	0
8	5	4	+1	1
9	7	9	−2	4
10	8	8	0	0
Sum of the deviations squared (Σd^2)				**20**

consequently Σd^2 will be larger. So the final formula used to calculate Spearman's rank order correlation coefficient takes into account the number of subjects and converts Σd^2 to a value between -1 and $+1$. As with Pearson's product moment correlation coefficient, a value of $+1$ represents a perfect positive correlation. A value of zero indicates the absence of any relationship, and -1 represents a perfect negative correlation. A p value will also be calculated to quantify the statistical significance of the correlation.

Chi-squares

A chi-square analysis is used to examine the frequency distribution of data across different groups. It enables a researcher to investigate whether a disproportionate number of subjects are located within one group as opposed to other groups. Researchers may be interested in whether adult males from a particular town (adult male population $= 10,000$) have a greater risk of heart disease than the national average. The researchers have gathered data on a nominal scale: this is where each individual is not ascribed a numerical value on a scale, instead they are given a category classification. In this case they are rated as very high risk, high risk, medium risk, low risk or very low risk, in terms of heart disease. The nationwide statistics reveal that 5 per cent of adult males are categorised as very high risk, 15 per cent as high risk, 35 per cent as medium risk, 35 per cent as low risk, and 10 per cent as very low risk. The researchers must also record how many of the town's adult male population fall into each category. Table 7.7 shows us the number of adult males who actually fall into each category within the town. This frequency distribution across risk categories for the town can then be compared to the frequency distribution for the whole country. This is done by converting the percentages for risk groups from the whole country into values relative to the population of the town. This would mean 5 per cent of the town's 10,000 strong adult male population would be placed in the high-risk category for the figures for the whole country.

The $O - E$ row represents the observed value minus the expected value. In this instance the observed value is the frequency seen in the town population. The expected value is the frequency that would be expected if the town adhered perfectly to the national frequency distribution. The $O - E$ row therefore provides a value for the extent to which the two frequency distributions are divergent. Note that the sum of all the $O - E$ values will always equal zero because there are 10,000 frequency counts in both the observed and the expected rows. Even though the distribution between categories may vary, resulting in some minus and some positive $O - E$ values, the total number is equal, which results in a total $O - E$ of zero. To convert all the $O - E$ values for each category to positive values, they are squared $(O - E^2)$. Each of these values is then divided by the expected frequency value for that category. For example, for the high-risk

Table 7.7 Frequency data for heart disease risk

Risk	Very high	High	Medium	Low	Very low	Total
Town	475	1480	3400	3455	990	10000
Whole country	500	1500	3500	3500	1000	10000
$O - E$	-25	-20	100	-45	-10	0
$O - E^2$	625	400	10000	2025	100	
$(O - E^2) / E$	1.25	0.27	2.86	0.58	0.10	**5.06**

category the $O - E^2$ value is 625. Dividing this by the expected value for the high risk category (500) gives a value of 1.25. All these values ($O - E^2 / E$) are then summed to give us the total of 5.06. This final figure is the chi-square value.

In a situation where the two category frequency distributions are perfectly matched (i.e. all the O and E figures for each category are identical), the chi-square value will be zero. However, had we drawn a sample of 10,000 adult males at random from across the whole country, it is unlikely that the frequency distribution across categories would have perfectly matched the frequency distribution of the whole country's adult male population. It is likely that there would be some discrepancies between the sample and the population category frequency distributions. In this case, the chi-square value occurring by chance alone would have been greater than zero. As with many of the statistical tests we have examined thus far, a researcher must compare the size of the value of the statistic they have calculated with the size of the statistic that might reasonably be expected to occur by chance in a randomly drawn sample. This process is again done with the use of a p value, telling us the probability of making a type I error. The alternate hypothesis for a chi square states that the expected category frequency distribution will differ from the observed distribution. The value of a chi-square distribution associated with a p value of 0.05 for this number of categories is 9.49. The value of 5.06 from the heart disease risk example is therefore not statistically significant at the $p < 0.05$ level. On the basis of these data alone, the researcher should accept the null hypothesis (that for adult men in the town, there is no difference in the frequency distribution for risk of heart disease between them and the country at large).

Chi-square analysis can also be applied to more complex experimental designs with more than one classification. In the heart disease risk example there was a single classification, which was the adult male population of the town, and there were five categories (very high risk, high risk, etc.). This design is referred to as a 1 × 5 design (one classification and five categories). It is possible to have more than one classification, as with a study that seeks to investigate differences in physique anxiety between adolescent males and females. In this study subjects were put into four categories indicating their perception of their own body. The four categories were: very content, content, dissatisfied, very dissatisfied. The design in this case has two classifications, male and female, making this a 2 × 4 design. The chi-square analysis will look for discrepancies in the category frequency distribution, between males and the expected distribution, and between females and the expected distribution. The expected category frequency distribution is ascertained by combining the frequency distributions for males and females (adding them together) and working out what percentage of the whole group falls in each category. The chi-square value for these more complex designs are also attributed a p value, which can be interpreted for statistical significance.

Limitations and assumptions of chi-squares

Chi-square analysis is biased towards large sample sizes. If you double the number of subjects, but keep proportionately the same category frequency distributions for both the observed and expected rows (i.e. doubling the frequency in each category), you will double the size of the chi-square value. This means that in very large samples, it is far easier to find a significant difference than in smaller samples. There is also a problem with small sample sizes, particularly when a large number of classifications and categories are used. The expected frequencies in each category, for each classification, should always be greater than one.

• When using samples to represent the frequency distribution of a wider population, samples should always be randomly selected.

SPSS guidance for non-parametric statistics

Procedures for carrying out non-parametric statistical procedures are covered in Chapter 19 of Coakes and Steed (2001).

Common mistakes

1 Not testing data for normality and applying parametric statistics to non-parametric data.
2 Using a non-parametric test for difference for independent samples, when the samples are dependent (repeated measures), or vice versa.
3 Performing a complex chi-square analysis with multiple classifications and categories, but too few subjects (see p. 99).

SUMMARY

The structure of non-parametric techniques is similar to their parametric equivalents. The notion of a p value still applies. The fundamental differences lie in the fact that the data are converted to an ordinal scale first. There are still tests of difference and tests of relationship, which serve the same purposes as parametric tests. Table 7.8 can be used to help you select the appropriate non-parametric statistical technique to use on your data.

Table 7.8 Selecting the right non-parametric test

	Statistical test		
	Go to Table 7.9	*Spearman's rank correlation*	*Chi-square*
Testing for difference	✓	✗	✗
Testing for relationships between variables	✗	✓	✗
Frequency data	✗	✗	✓

Table 7.9 Non-parametric tests of difference

	Statistical test			
	Mann-Whitney U test	*Wilcoxon signed rank test*	*Kruskal-Wallis ANOVA*	*Friedman test*
Only two samples	✓	✓	✗	✗
Independent samples	✓	✗	✓	✗
Dependent samples	✗	✓	✗	✓

8

PRESENTATION OF DATA

If a research project is not worth doing at all, it is not worth doing properly.

Anon

LEARNING OUTCOMES

Following this chapter you should be able to:

1 understand the importance of presenting data;
2 present data precisely, concisely and appropriate to the task;
3 evaluate strengths and weaknesses of presented data.

Prior to reading this chapter you should have had some experience with the following:

- writing a literature review or report
- constructing tables and figures
- analysing data.

Introduction

Throughout your programme of study, you will probably have been asked either to find data from textbooks or to generate data in the laboratory. By 'data', we mean information that can be ascribed a value, whether that value is assessed as a nominal, ordinal, interval or ratio scale, and by which we begin to make inferences (see Chapters 4–6). In some instances you will have been asked to present these data in class and this might have resulted in your formulating some tables or graphs. Whilst the task of finding the data from other references or generating it in the laboratory may seem harder than formulating a table, poorly constructed tables or graphs can ruin much of the hard work performed by the student.

The fundamental principle that should be adhered when dealing with the presentation of data is *communication*. The appropriate form of communication to your audience will ensure them of your confidence in the subject matter that you are dealing with. Contrast two hypothetical situations of students presenting data. The first student presents data that are disorganised, following no logical structure, and has attempted to fit everything onto one sheet of paper or overhead transparency. The second student, having thought about the most important elements to the data set, selects the most relevant data, arranges the data logically and spaces the data appropriately, perhaps over several sheets of paper. All things being equal, the second presentation of data would be much easier to comprehend and, from the audience's or your lecturer's perspective, should cause much less anxiety in trying to decipher what has been accomplished. In summary, presentation of data is about condensing all the raw data, presenting an informative summary by focusing on the most important details of the data.

The presentation of data can be arranged into three forms:

1 text
2 tables
3 figures.

The most important decision to be made when presenting data in a report or thesis is to choose which format should be used for which data. Although there are no definitive rules, there are some guidelines to allow you to make an informed choice. It is important to try to minimise overlap between these three forms of presentation. In a report or dissertation it would be pointless to have the same information represented as a table and a figure. Usually you have to adhere to a strict word count, so this would represent an unnecessary waste of space and words. Also think about the reader: they do not wish to have read the same information twice. So in order not to waste everyone's time, avoid replication of the data set within text and graphical form. Once you have decided on the appropriate presentation method, ensure that there is informative and consistent use of titles and labelling. The title should be explicit but descriptive and should not take the form of a question or statement. Also ensure that all references to units are explicitly explained and do not confuse the reader as to what was measured. It is usual to place the title below the figures but above the tables. If there are specific conventions within your programme, then these should be adhered to, but either way the emphasis is on a consistency of approach by the author for the benefit of the reader.

Guidelines for text

In a report or dissertation the presentation of data in text form is most usually found in the results section, although data from other studies can be presented in either the introduction or literature review. However, wherever data are found, the following should be adhered to. The first guideline is to keep text to a minimum: do not interpret the data, merely provide a description/commentary. This is because it is the purpose of the discussion section to comment more critically on the data. The saying 'a picture is worth a thousand words' is a very apt one in this respect. As a general rule, if you can present data in tables, schematics or figures then do so. The problem with data presented as text, is that it can require a lot of words to explain what all the data represent. The use of text, in a results section is more useful for presenting results of statistical tests, for example:

> Figure 1.1 compares the predicted $\dot{V}O_2$ values at each stage of the test to those measured in the student and client groups. The student t tests revealed statistically significant differences ($p < 0.05$) between the predicted values and those obtained from the students for all stages compared. The p values for stages 4 to 8 respectively were 0.02, 0.018, 0.013, 0.011 and 0.01. Statistical differences

were identified between the predicted values and the client group for stages 3 (P = 0.045), 4 (p = 0.041), 6 (p = 0.032) and 7 (p = 0.023).

In the above example very specific reference has been made to the statistical significance and the incorporation of a description of the data, i.e. the average and standard deviation. In the results section it is becoming usual to report the exact p values as it allows the reader to interpret results. When using text to present data apart from the statistical significance, try to pick out trends in the data. Similarly try to select important or surprising data as this can demonstrate your ability to evaluate the data and attach importance to it.

Also when reporting data ensure that there is consistency with decimal places and that the number of decimal places does not exceed the accuracy of the instrument. For example, a student once wrote in a report that the average stature of the group was 178.3478 ± 9.7835 cm. The implication of this lack of appreciation for precision was that the student was able to measure stature to 1/10000 cm. This is a common mistake in student work, most likely due to the ability of spreadsheets and statistical programmes to compute numbers to the nth decimal place and the student's willingness merely to copy it down. Therefore, take time to consider how precisely you can measure a variable and whether by presenting the data to multiple decimal places you are trying to convey greater precision than is possible.

When representing data in text format it is important to ensure that a unit of measure always accompanies a numeral. For example, a student might write that the stature of the 15 hockey players was 177 ± 9 but neglect to include the fact that the symbol for centimetres, cm, should have been included after the standard deviation figure. This mistake is often made because the student assumes that as they have indicated it is a stature measurement, everyone will know that the unit of measure is centimetres. However, it is possible that a lecturer could play devil's advocate and state it should be in metres! Therefore, to remove any ambiguities, always include the units of measure after the numeral.

Another common problem when presenting data in text form is when there is a series of different groups and different variables to be described. It is common practice to use the word 'respectively' to highlight the order of the data. For example, a sentence might state 'the peak power of the male and female athletes was 889 ± 150 and 591 ± 110 W respectively'. The use of this phrase indicates the first numerals refer to the males and the second set to the females. Clearly when there are more than two groups, care must be taken that the meaning of the sentence is not lost with all the numbers; it might be better to bracket the numbers after the descriptor. For example, 'the peak power of the hockey players (890 ± 137 W), football players (830 ± 129 W) and rugby players (950 ± 169 W) was significantly different ($p < 0.05$)'.

Guidelines for tables

Tables are an ideal format to contain specific information in a relatively small space, yet can convey much summative information for the benefit of the reader. I encourage all students to use tables as it is very easy to order the data and the student invariably gets a very comprehensive 'feel' for the data. Tables are often useful for summarising group data (means, standard deviations). Therefore, tables are an effective way to present descriptive statistics. Probably the only time *not* to use a table would be if you only had three or four means and standard deviations (e.g., age, stature and body mass) and the information was simplistic. In this case it would be more appropriate to write it in text rather than going to the effort of constructing a table.

In Table 8.1 a summary data table has been constructed to represent shoulder flexibility data of rugby players. Example A shows a poorly constructed table and Example B shows how with some re-arrangement the same information can be more effectively presented.

When constructing tables, only relevant material is included and both text and numerals are kept to a minimum. This has the effect of reducing what could be a very crowded table. First, avoid the temptation to include everything, as it will make it harder for the reader to understand what the table represents. Tables that are cluttered will only frustrate the reader, often resulting in their not reading that section. Second, note the limited use of lines to outline the table. Wherever possible avoid multiple uses of horizontal and vertical lines and boxes within a table. It is easier on the eye if just horizontal lines are used. Therefore, it is important that you space the data appropriately, do not clutter numerals and text on top of one another. Third, note that the title comes at the top and is specific. It is also usual to write the title of both figures and

Table 8.1 A poorly constructed table (Example A) in comparison to a more effective and well presented table (Example B)

Example A

Mean scores for front row

no	shldr flex	shldr ext
6	150	35.6

Mean scores for the second row

n	shldr flex	shldr ext
4	160.6	59

Mean scores for the back row

no	shldr flex	shldr ext
6	155	57.2

Mean scores for the scrum halves

no	shldr flex	shldr ext
2	121	45

Mean scores for the fly halves

no	shldr flex	shldr ext
3	153.8	32.4

Example B: Shoulder flexibility (Mean SD) according to position

Position	N	Flexion (°)	Extension (°)
Front row	6	150 ± 4	36 ± 6
Second row	4	161 ± 6	59 ± 7
Back row	6	155 ± 4	57 ± 4
Half backs	5	130 ± 6	49 ± 5
Centres	5	154 ± 7	33 ± 6
Wings/Full Backs	6	143 ± 4	59 ± 4

tables in italic or bold text. This practice helps differentiate between the text and the title.

Guidelines for figures (graphs and schematics)

In this section graphs are included under the heading 'figures' because other presentations such as schematics are often used to present data or information and so to avoid having to write Graph 1, Graph 2, Schematic 1, Schematic 2 and Schematic 3, the descriptor 'Figure' is used inclusively. Graphs are ideal for seeing patterns or trends in the data. By plotting data, it is possible to observe the shape of the curves and therefore aid interpretation. When you plot data in a graph, ensure the title goes beneath the graph, and again it should be specific to what is contained within the figure. A common mistake made by students is the incorrect labelling of the axes and units. Often the axes might be labelled but the units of the measure are omitted. Also with regard to the axes, ensure the scale of the units is appropriate, don't use misleading scales, and if the scale is very large, use breaks in axes where appropriate. Preferably, the axes should always start at 0 as this prevents distortion of the pattern of the data, but breaks in the axes will overcome this problem.

As a minimum, a figure must contain a title, information regarding the units of measure, and labelling on the axes. It is conventional practice to place the independent variable (the cause) on the x-axis and the dependent variable (the effect) on the y-axis.

In Figure 8.1a a graph has been constructed to show how badly a graph can be plotted just through a lack of detail. Opposite is the same figure (8.1b), which has been corrected to show how much more effective the figure is at presenting the data. By amending five main areas the graph has been transformed. First, the title has been amended to reflect what the data is representing, i.e. the relationship between maximal lactate steady state and running speed. Instead of the title being written as a statement it describes the data. The second and third changes have been made to the x-axis and a more logical division of the data for running speed and the unit of measure for speed in km.h^{-1} have been created. The change to the y-axis has ensured the appropriate units of measure for blood lactate and the label is easily read by being placed horizontally. Lastly, the regression line of the data has been added and the regression statistics positioned near the regression so that it is obvious what the figures represent.

If you have a complex graph, think about splitting it up into several graphs. This will prevent having to cram a lot of complex information into one area and will prevent confusing the reader. When selecting a particular type of graph it is useful to consider the type of data you are representing. For example, if it is frequency data then a histogram, or pie chart for percentages can be used. Pie charts are particularly useful if you are showing the relative proportions amongst different groups. Alternatively if the collected data attempted to investigate a relationship between two variables, then a scatter plot would be best used. If the presented data is trying to show the difference between two groups then a bar chart, using standard error of the mean as error bars rather than SD, could be used. Data collected across time are probably best represented by a line graph with similar reference to the standard error of the mean. If your figure has many plot symbols and labels, it is always better to label them directly rather than placing them into a legend. This is for two reasons: first, it avoids the reader having to constantly cross-check from the legend back to the figure and vice versa. If there are

Figure 8.1a 10K running performance depends on lactate steady-state

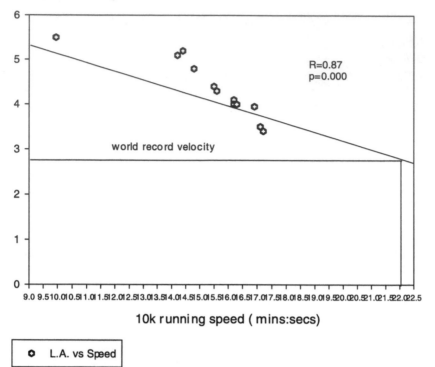

Figure 8.1a 10K running performance depends on lactate steady-state
Reproduced courtesy of Prof. Jo Doust

many labels this can be tedious. Second, the more labels there are, the more cluttered the legend box becomes. However, you must also be careful not to clutter the figure with labels and plot symbols all over, as this too can become distracting. The other common mistake students make when presenting data is using 3-D for figures. Although different packages like Excel and Sigmaplot can produce these effects, they often confuse the reader rather than aiding their understanding. Also, reading numerals off the axes of a 3-D figure is more difficult than in a 2-D figure. Most journals do not publish 3-D figures, so follow their rejection of them and avoid their use.

Table 8.2 and Figures 8.2–8.4 are examples of how data can be re-organised and formatted differently. In Table 8.2, $\dot{V}O_2$ scores, which have been predicted and then measured for students and clients, have been placed in a table. Although the table is correctly constructed, by using a figure (Figure 8.2) the same data is much more effectively visualised.

In the figure, it is easier to see the trends. The figure also has a more effective impact and is likely to aid interpretation. Also note that in Figure 8.3 information that appears cluttered in a pie chart is much more effective when placed in a bar graph. The pattern is much easier to spot, e.g. satisfaction scores 2, 3 and 4 are similar, whilst satisfaction scores 5 and 6 form the next cluster and then scores 7 and 8 have the highest percentage

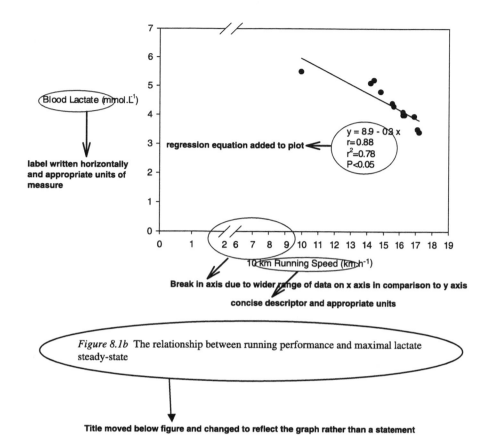

Figure 8.1b The relationship between running performance and maximal lactate steady-state

Table 8.2 Visualising results of analysis

Comparison of predicted and measured oxygen uptake at each stage of a maximal oxygen uptake test

Stage	Speed $(m·s^{-1})$	Grade (%)	Predicted $\dot{V}O_2$ $(mL·kg^{-1}·min^{-1})$	Student $\dot{V}O_2$ $(mL·kg^{-1}·min^{-1})$	Client $\dot{V}O_2$ $(mL·kg^{-1}·min^{-1})$
2	0.89	0	8.9		8.3 ± 0.5
3	1.11	0	10.2		8.6 ± 0.5*
4	1.34	0	11.5	8.9 ± 0.4*	10.3 ± 0.4*
5	1.56	0	12.9	9.5 ± 0.5*	12.9 ± 0.3
6	1.56	3	17.9	11.6 ± 0.5*	15.5 ± 0.4*
7	1.56	3	23.0	13.9 ± 0.6*	18.6 ± 0.7*
8	1.56	9	28.1	17.4 ± 0.9*	

of satisfaction scores. Biomechanical data, which often involve many data points, can be very difficult to analyse, and may therefore create difficulties when deciding to plot the data. In Figure 8.4 heel inversion angle against time has been plotted but in the first graph the poor identification of what the lines represent and lack of any identification symbols make it very difficult to appreciate what the plot is representing. The second

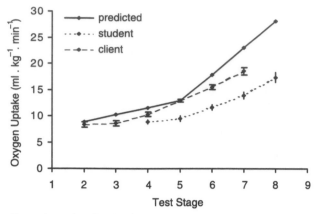

Comparison of predicted and measured oxygen uptake at each stage of the test

Figure 8.2 Visualising results of analysis
Reproduced courtesy of Dr. Martin Bailey

graph has differentiated between asymptomatic and symptomatic participants. The use of error bars has also been included to show the variability around each of the data points.

Presentations

In many programmes related to sport and exercise, students are required to perform an oral or poster presentation as part of a seminar programme or assessment. The same principle still applies for both these presentations as stated previously, namely the primacy *communication*. In the oral presentation you often have a time limit, therefore it is important that you are able to communicate to the audience all the relevant information needed to achieve your purpose. The poster presentation does not always involve a time limit but the amount of information is limited and determined by the area of the board upon which your poster is attached. Following some of the useful hints and tips below will ensure that you make an effective presentation.

Oral presentations

If you participate in an oral presentation that requires data to be presented, then there are three important questions to be answered:

- What is the purpose of the oral presentation?
- Who are the target audience?
- What information needs to be presented?

The next piece of information you will need is the duration of the oral. If a 10-minute presentation is required, one of the main problems with such a short presentation is knowing what to omit, whereas with a longer presentation (e.g. 30 minutes), this is not as important. To ensure that the data are adequately presented, there are a number of factors to consider:

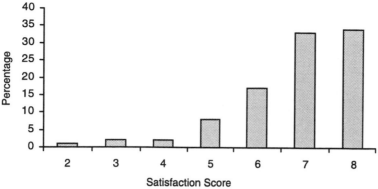

Proportion of customers in each scoring category on the satisfaction questionnaires

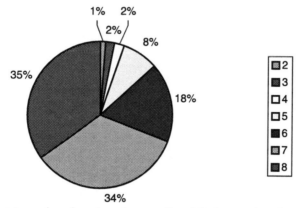

Proportion of customers in each scoring category on the satisfaction questionnaires

Figure 8.3 Use of graphs 1

Reproduced courtesy of Dr. Martin Bailey

1   The size of the Table or Figure. If you are using a powerpoint presentation then the *minimum* font size you need is **18**. You should remember that when your slides are projected up on a wall screen they will not look exactly as they do on the computer screen.

2   Do not try to present too much data on any one slide. It is far better to have a number of slides of data rather than cram everything onto one.

3   Take your time presenting the data. If presenting data via a figure, you can highlight the axes, the symbols or any particular data points you want to emphasise by pointing to them. Similarly, if presenting data via a table, highlight the horizontal variables and the vertical variables and then point out specific data e.g. specific means and standard deviations. Usually you have access to a laser pointer or the room might be small enough that you can physically point to the relevant data or title.

4   There is no need to label figures or tables as Figure 1 or 2, or Table 1 or 2, in an oral presentation, but each should possess an appropriate title.

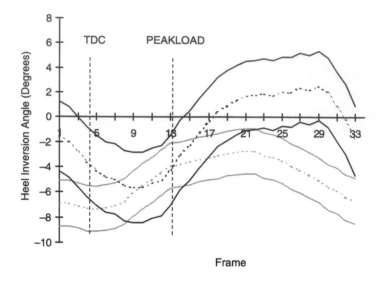

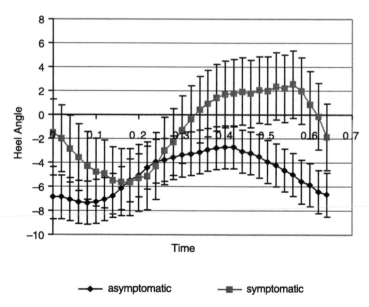

—◆— asymptomatic   —■— symptomatic

Figure 8.4 Use of graphs 2

Reproduced courtesy of Dr. Martin Bailey

5   Show informative descriptive statistics (means, SDs, frequencies, proportions, correlations, effect sizes) but there is no need to show the test statistics, e.g. t, F.

6   In general, people find figures easier to decipher than tables and it is certainly easier to show trends and outliers. Therefore, ensure that all symbols are clear, use colour if necessary to differentiate between several variables. However, take care with the use of colours as not only are some people colour blind but certain

colours such as purple and blue can merge together and be indistinguishable from one another.

Poster presentations

Poster presentations are an effective means to present your data as there is usually no time limit; however, you are limited by space requirements on the board upon which the poster is pinned. Many of the points discussed above in the oral presentation are also relevant for the poster. These include:

- *The use of colour* – posters should stand out so be willing to make an impact with your layout.
- *Font size* – consider the font size of the presented data: can the poster be read from about 1 metre away? Use as a minimum 24 point font.
- *Choice of format* – posters are ideal for presenting data in a variety of tables and figures so consider carefully which formats have most visual impact.

Because a poster presentation is invariably displayed for a considerably longer time than an oral presentation, other readers will have a lot longer to inspect your work. Therefore, you must take care to ensure that tables and figures are correctly presented. These include the labelling of axes, units of measures, use of symbols and the appropriate use of numerals to indicate accuracy of the variables. However, as you often get the opportunity to talk to more people with a poster, you can engage the audience in a more constructive conversation related to your work. Nowadays, it is possible to format a poster through PowerPoint and have it printed out as one complete large sheet poster. If you unable to do this, then using PowerPoint and printing individual A4 sheets which are laminated can be just as effective. Remember the presentation of the data will never replace the substance of the question and rationale of the project but presented effectively it will enhance an already well-thought-out and conducted project.

Common mistakes

1 The construction of a table with too little or simplistic data. Simple results should have been written as text.
2 Too much material in a table or figure. If necessary use an appendix or appendices to present the raw data. The presentation of raw data can often help a lecturer go through your analyses if you happen to have made mistakes. By checking the raw data, mistakes can be prevented from being repeated.
3 Inappropriate use of scaling on axes and lack of information related to the labels and units of a figure.
4 Font sizes too small.
5 Too many colours in a presentation.
6 Too many formats and a neglect for the scientific content.
7 PowerPoint presentations which use too many gizmos.

SUMMARY

Wherever data are presented in either the results section or a literature review, the main aim is to be as concise and precise as possible. This not only applies to the actual presentation of the text, table or figure with its formatting style, but also to the presentation of the actual data in terms of scientific convention. Allocate as much time as you devote to the discussion or the literature review. This will reflect the precision of your work as a sport or exercise scientist.

9

INTERPRETATION OF DATA

Far better an approximate answer to the right question, which is often vague, than the exact answer to the wrong question which can also be precise.

John W. Tukey (1915–2000)

LEARNING OUTCOMES

Following this chapter you should be able to:

1   understand the association between the analysis of the data and its interpretation;
2   interpret data in the context of its strengths and weaknesses.

Prior to reading this chapter you should have had some experience with the following:

* analysing data
* presenting data in a variety of formats
* formulating a research or project question.

Introduction

The interpretation of the data is always considered in the discussion section of a report or dissertation. In fact, many students make the mistake of discussing some of the data in the results section. This must be avoided: like the methods section, the results should only describe the data, without any explanation. Otherwise the reader will have difficulty in referring back and forth between two sections in an effort to try to understand what you have found and why. The discussion section differs because you are attempting to relate the data to the objectives of the project. This means that you must critically evaluate the relationships, try to qualify the objectives, expand them where necessary, draw inferences and evaluate findings. It is fundamentally different to the results section, where you have just attempted to help the reader in understanding the data by describing general trends, highlighting differences and/or similarities amongst the data points. Therefore, it is vital that you are able to show the reader that you have expertise with the data and demonstrate your ability to discuss results critically and promote your research skills.

In this chapter the interpretation of the data is the culmination of all the hard work that has gone into thinking about the problem, devising the question and/or hypotheses, designing the experiment, collecting and analysing the data. If you get the interpretation of the data right, then you are likely to score well in your assignment. If you perform poorly at the interpretation stage, it will demonstrate that you are competent at proposing a question and devising an experiment and collecting the data, but that you are unable to critique the data in relation to the question.

As this is the culmination of all your hard work, it would be advantageous to refer back to Chapters 4–7 and ensure that you are fully familiar with the different statistical techniques. If you are confident with the statistical techniques, then you will be able to interpret the data much more effectively. However, it is not just a case of concentrating on the statistics; often these are relied on too much. In Chapter 6 one of the first things that you were recommended to do was to plot the data and visually inspect it – by doing so you should begin to get an idea of the pattern of the measured variables. Aside from the reliance on statistics, there is another technique to use and that is *common sense*. Too often students believe that because their statistics do not show significance, their project has failed. This is far from the truth. Conversely, many students bask in the glory of statistical significance as if this were somehow the overseer of a job well done. Students must realise that statistics do not make or break a project. Rather, it is *you*, as the sport or exercise scientist, and your ability to communicate what you have done, why you have done it, and what you have found and why, that will be the ultimate determinant of the quality of your work. A famous quote can serve as a timely warning of what *not* to do:

'He uses statistics as a drunken man uses lampposts – for support rather than illumination' (Andrew Lang 1844–1912). Therefore, you must use the statistics to illuminate your arguments but provide the support from your knowledge and understanding of the topic to critically discuss the results in as scientific and applied a manner as possible.

Generic information related to the interpretation of data

Before you start to interpret the data, here is a checklist to ensure that you can interpret the data meaningfully:

1 Do you fully understand what type of data (nominal, ordinal, interval or ratio) you have collected?
2 Do you understand the units of measurement that the data represent?
3 Have you checked the range and magnitude of the data?
4 Have you double-checked that the data collected are able to answer your hypotheses?
5 Have you got any outliers or data points that do not look right? If so, check them out.
6 Were you aware of any problems during the data collection stage?
7 Are you confident the data were reliably collected?

If you are able to deal with each of these questions, then you should feel confident to begin to interpret your data.

Difference testing

Interpreting effects

If there is one difficulty that students have when it comes to interpreting statistics, it is related to the tests of differences and whether the results are significant or not. However, do not despair because even postgraduates, sport and exercise science lecturers and many others grapple with this issue. The problem partly resides in the fact that many students undertake an obligatory statistics course where t tests and ANOVAs are taught and, in particular, the ubiquitous use of the statistically significant p value. After this course, students armed with this knowledge heap so much importance on the determination of statistical significance that they often forget everything else.

An effect is an outcome and researchers are interested in generalising from the observed value and translating this to a 'true (but always unknown) value' of the whole population. The only way you would ever know the 'true value' would be to sample the whole population! In most cases this is clearly impractical. In students' work it is often written that the treatment had no effect on the dependent variable and therefore the null hypothesis was accepted. However, it should be highlighted that it is highly unlikely that effects on dependent variables will ever be zero – there will always be some sort of effect (including the possibility of zero). The question is: how significant is the effect both in terms of the statistical and practical interpretation? For this process of interpreting the size of the effect, we can use Cohen's descriptors for small, moderate and large effect sizes. These descriptors for the effect size equate to 0.2, 0.5 and 0.8 but must be used with caution (Cohen 1988). Other authors have suggested a broader range of qualitative descriptors and figures to help interpret effect sizes (Hopkins 2000). For further discussion about this topic, students are encouraged to read Hopkins, Hawley and Burke (1999).

How significant is significant?

One of the main problems for sport and exercise science students is this term 'significant'. Such is its hold over students that many will say that if their results are non-significant, then their study has been a failure. This is not necessarily the case. It is entirely possible to achieve statistically significant results and for those results to have no importance or meaning whatsoever. It is only because students have developed misguided confidence in the statistical significance of the results.

Even amongst statisticians there is widespread debate about the purpose and meaning of the term 'significant'. Many statisticians advocate that it should be replaced with a descriptor like 'discernible' and that this would convey a much clearer interpretation as to what the results have shown (Wonnacott 1987: 261). However, if we accept for the moment the continued use of the word 'significance', a common occurrence is that some students view some p values as being more significant than other p values. It is not uncommon to read students' work that states a p value of 0.004 is more significant than another p value of 0.01. However, if a threshold value of $p < 0.05$ is set prior to the calculation of the statistics, this perspective would be incorrect. Why? It is because once a threshold is set, if it is less than $p < 0.05$ then it doesn't matter whether it is below by a considerable margin or just under, the decision is that the result is statistically significant. Now this approach is not flawless: if one p value is 0.052 and another is 0.048, you might declare the former insignificant and the latter significant. This approach to significance testing is meant to allow a yes/no decision-making process without any grey areas, but is this fair? The results that are defined as statistically non-significant might actually be worthy of closer examination. Owing to the implications of such a strict and rigid approach, there is an alternative strategy.

One alternative approach is to cite the actual p value in your report or dissertation and allow the readers to interpret the p value for themselves. Therefore, in a report the author might cite the p values for a particular test as significant (p = 0.02). This has led to a situation where some writers are using an adjective such as 'very' significant (p = 0.001) to describe the p values. Whatever the merits of this format of description, the interpretation of the statistics must be closely allied to the discussion of the scientific theory, and it is largely irrelevant as to the descriptors used before the word significant.

There is one scenario that has not be discussed fully so far and that is when non-significance is attained. In many cases of undergraduate projects this is a real possibility, not necessarily because the project was unreliable or poorly conducted but because the project did not have enough statistical power. As a result of financial and time constraints, most student projects will consist of small subject numbers, therefore the experimental design's ability to detect a difference is likely to be reduced. Power is the probability of correctly rejecting a false null hypothesis and is influenced by the type I and type II error and the sample size. In student projects, even if there is a discernible difference between two groups, if the sample size is small then the probability of correctly rejecting a false null hypothesis is decreased (Figure 9.1).

Practical versus statistical significance

Exercise and sport scientists often want to know whether the treatment had an effect, or what the probability is that the treatment has had an effect, given the data. The statistician pursues this question differently and presents the probability of getting this result given the treatment has no effect. In other words, the scientist and the statistician are pursuing the answer to a question but from opposite sides: both are connected but are not the same.

However, one of the first questions you should ask is 'is there a practical difference?' If there is practical difference, then even if there is not a statistical one, the practical difference could be large enough to be meaningful in the real world. For example, a study is conducted to investigate the claims of a new sports drink on 3000-metre running performance. A double blind randomised cross-over design with the drink and a placebo is employed with sufficient power to detect meaningful differences, and it is found that participants improve their run time by 20 seconds; however, it is not statistically significant. But in the context of the 3000-metre running performance, this 20 seconds difference could relate to the participant moving closer to the medal winning positions. It is important that students establish a balanced opinion in their interpretation of the data and do not become solely focused on the establishment of statistical significance. Of course, if you can establish a practical difference which is both meaningful in the real world and statistically significant, then you are likely to have found meaningful outcomes.

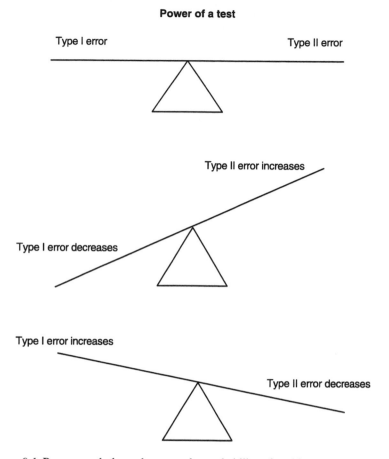

Figure 9.1 Power as a balance between the probability of making a type I and type II error

Summary

The significance of an experiment both in terms of the statistics and its practicalities will often be interpreted in relation to an applied setting. Therefore, it is important that students do not become too preoccupied with statistical significance or insignificance. This is merely one part of your argument. It is entirely conceivable that statistically insignificant results can have real practical meaning and that the explanations and judgements you make in discussing the data will add to the relevance of your results and the hypotheses that you have set.

Correlation studies

Cause and effect?

In Chapter 3 it was stated that correlational studies are the weakest experimental design if you are trying to establish cause and effect. Therefore, your interpretation of the data must keep this fact in mind. Many students still forget and begin to infer beyond the scope of the data, concluding that there is a cause and effect between two variables. For example, if we correlate pizza consumption and age, we will probably get a linear positive correlation. Although we could postulate that age is an independent factor and is causing the increase in pizza consumption, it could equally be as a result of the greater spending power of the consumer as they age.

The size of the correlation

Any two variables correlated against each other will produce some sort of correlation even if it is zero. Therefore one of the important factors related to correlations is the size of the correlation. A correlation could be statistically significant yet be of the magnitude of $r = 0.20$. Hence the size of the correlation is important, either negative or positive, because it describes the strength of the relationship between the variables. The strength of the relationship between two variables can be expressed as a percentage. For example, if a correlation was found between two variables of $r = 0.91$, then by squaring 0.91 and multiplying by 100, we have r^2 or variance explained. This is known as the coefficient of determination. In this example the variance explained is 81 per cent. Therefore, 81 per cent of the variance in Y is explained by the X variable (see page 84). Hopefully you can appreciate that the closer the correlation is to 1.0, the greater is the explained variance between the two variables. This common variance can also be used as a predictor, in other words the variance in one variable predicts 81 per cent of the variance in the other variable. It is therefore easy to understand, once we start using correlations in the context of prediction, how students misinterpret cause and effect.

One question often asked is how to qualify the size of a correlation. For example, is a correlation of 0.58 small, moderate or big? A statistician by the name of Jacob Cohen has provided us with a criterion guide to qualifying the size of the correlations. He defined a correlation of 0.5 as large, 0.3 as moderate and 0.1 as small. However, there are other qualifiers in the literature, which describe 0.7 as very large, 0.9 as nearly perfect and 1.0 as perfect. Take care not to confuse these qualifiers for the correlation coefficient with those of the effect size mentioned earlier.

In most physiology and biomechanics studies, because the predictive powers of variables are often investigated, correlations invariably need to be greater than 0.80 to act as an effective predictor. In psychology, correlations, particularly from questionnaires, are often interpreted differently. Due to the nature of the variables and the precision of the instruments, it is not uncommon for psychologists to accept lower correlations ($r = 0.5–0.7$ are not untypical) as being practically useful. Therefore, the correlations must be interpreted in context to each situation. In some medical studies, correlations as low as 0.2 were found to be meaningful and relevant.

The range of the data

One of the weaknesses of correlation is that it is dependent on the range of the data for both the X and Y variable. For example, if both the X and Y variable have an equal and large range (and both are interval data), then the correlation will be higher than if one variable were a nominal variable and the other were an interval variable. Similarly, if you have a group of students whose range of body mass is restricted between 50–80 kg (Figure 9.2a) correlated with their stature, the obtained correlation is 0.57. Afterwards

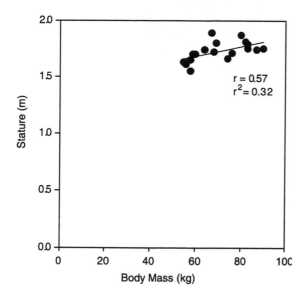

Figure 9.2a A correlation coefficient with a constricted Y variable of a group of students

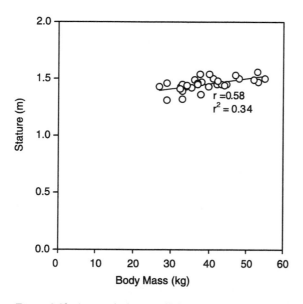

Figure 9.2b A correlation coefficient with a constricted Y variable of a group of children

you decide to test some children as well for body mass and stature and obtain a similar correlation r = 0.58 (Figure 9.2b).

However, if you add the data together (hence producing a much wider spread of scores for both stature and body mass) the correlation is much stronger, r = 0.90 (Figure 9.3). Therefore, the correlation is strongly influenced by the range of the X and Y scores. Although this restriction leads to the lowering of the correlation coefficient, in

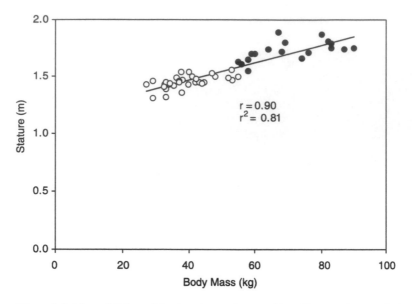

Figure 9.3 The addition of further data points and its effect on the correlation coefficient

certain disciplines such as psychology, techniques have been used to correct for a restriction in the range of the data.

Other factors that can affect the interpretation of data are the effect of an outlier on the correlation statistic. Using the above example of body mass and stature measurements, if the tester was new to the techniques of measuring stature and body mass and measured three subjects wrongly (remember, human error is a threat to reliability), then the correlation is reduced, r = −0.48 (Figure 9.4). Note that not only is it reduced, but also the correlation has been transformed from a positive to a negative correlation. Consider also that despite the negative correlation, as a result of the squaring of the correlation, the correlation of determination is always positive. In Figure 9.4 the tester had mistakenly recorded the three data points as 177, 165 and 155 kg instead of 77, 65 and 55 kg. This is why a visual inspection of the data is always encouraged, but how you decide to interpret the outliers is an important issue. In this example it would have been easy to visually spot the mistake and change the data. However, if the three data points had been real scores perhaps taken from obese patients, then a decision would have to be made regarding whether these outliers were left in the analyses. Often outliers present some of the most interesting data for you to discuss, so do not merely discard them from your analyses for no other reason than that they influence your statistics.

Statistical versus practical significance

Although a correlation can be statistically significant, it does not mean that it is of any practical use. In the above example of the medical studies, low correlations were found that would be classified as small but the practical interpretation of the data was sufficient to allow the researchers to develop the project further. Therefore, always consider the practical significance: for example, if two variables correlate 0.50 does a r^2 of 25 per cent help to predict the variance of one variable to the other? If this prediction is

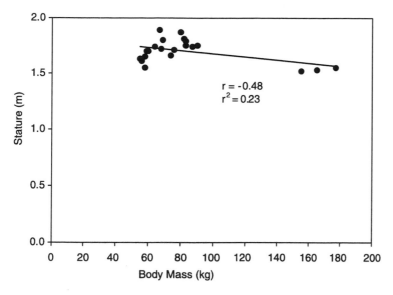

Figure 9.4 The effect of three outliers on the correlation coefficient

useful then the statistical significance becomes less important. Of course, what the statistic cannot tell you is which 25 per cent of the variance will affect the Y variable.

Common mistakes

The important key points to interpreting correlational studies are:

1 Assuming that findings are a proof of cause and effect. Many factors influence the biomechanical, physiological and psychological variables studied in sport and exercise science, therefore correlations should be interpreted with caution as additional variables could be also be responsible for the calculated correlation coefficient.
2 A failure to understand that there is always a relationship between two variables.
3 A misinterpretation between the statistical importance of the p value and the size of the correlation and its practical meaning.
4 A lack of the appropriate correlation statistic, particularly where one variable is nominal or ordinal and the other is an interval variable.

Regression analyses

Prediction or cause and effect?

A natural extension of correlational analyses is regression. It should not be too difficult to appreciate that if you can plot two variables on a scatter plot, and calculate the correlation coefficient, then you can go one step further and predict the Y score from X score. In predicting one variable from scores of another variable, it should be remembered that that is just what you are performing, a *prediction*. With any prediction there may be error. The aim is to obtain a model with the minimum error. One way to achieve this is to use two variables as closely correlated as possible, hence the shared variance between the two variables will be high. As regression analysis is concerned with prediction, just like correlation analysis, cause and effect must not be assumed. Therefore, confine your conclusions to issues related to the strength of the relationship, the ability to predict and the amount of error that the analyses produce.

The prediction model

From Chapter 6 regression analysis was introduced and providing the assumptions related to the normality, homogeneity, spread and outliers related to the data are understood, there are a number of other important points that will aid you in interpreting the data. The first one is to assess the regression equation derived from the prediction model. Remember, the stronger the correlation coefficient, then the greater the predictive ability. However, as mentioned previously, in order to qualify how accurate the model is at predicting performance, the standard error of estimate (SE_E) should be examined (see Chapter 6). By equating the SE_E to the predictor variable, you will be able to make a qualitative judgement as to whether the model is useful to predict the average value of the Y variable. For example, if a health scientist believes that someone who has weak back muscle also has weak abdominal muscle, a test of abdominal strength might be used in order to predict back strength. This might be useful for low back pain sufferers who might be unwilling to maximally test their back muscles because of back pain. If the model produces a SE_E of 25 N·m and a mean score of the predictor variable is 100 N·m, then we can say with 68 per cent confidence that the actual score will be ±25 N·m or ±1 SE_E. This margin of error might be too high to be of any practical use and therefore the health scientist might wish to measure another independent variable in order to improve the SE_E.

If the model produces a SE_E that has a low margin of error in relation to the predictor variable, then this can be interpreted as a positive indicator of the regression model. However, you must consider several important points. First, this model is really only valid for the sample that you have collected the data on. However, in real life, many models are published from which scientists use the regression equation to predict a variable. For example, many skinfold equations have been devised to predict and estimate body fat percentage. If a prediction equation is used, check how the model was formulated. Check who the sample subjects were, the age of the subjects and how the data was collected. Second, the model should be checked for the spread or range of the data because once the model is used to predict beyond the original data set, then errors could be increased. The establishment of one X variable, which has a strong predictive power of another variable, does not mean that a different X variable will be equally strong or stronger in predicting the Y variable.

Once a single X variable has been used to predict a Y variable, students often wish to extend this model to use other X variables to improve the predictive powers of the regression equation. Earlier, in Chapter 6, reference was made to how multiple regression can be used to measure numerous X variables in order to predict the Y variable (see p. 89). If a coefficient of determination (r^2) is 60 per cent ($r^2 = 0.60$) and the addition of a second variable to the model improves the r^2 to 90 per cent, then most students would agree that the measurement of this second variable is a worthwhile addition to the regression equation. However, if you added a third variable and the r^2 increased to

93 per cent, it is worth asking whether this is a worthwhile contribution to the equation. Students often include numerous additional variables, which make little further contribution to the predictive power of the regression model. If this is the case, then consider whether the extra trouble it will take to measure these additional variables is actually worth the effort. Would a more sensible approach be to just include the two main independent variables, which contribute the largest amount to the predictive power of the equation?

If this common-sense approach is ignored and numerous additional variables are included, a violation of the number of additional variables to the number of subjects can occur. That is, for every additional X variable in the model there should be at least five subjects and typically a subject to variable ratio of 20:1 is suggested. A further violation of regression analyses occurs when additional independent variables are included into the multiple regression because of the intercorrelation that often occurs between these independent variables. If possible, the addition of second and third X variables should be on the basis that they are correlated as little as possible with each other. This issue is known as collinearity. For example, stature and body mass are interrelated and will result in a more difficult task of interpreting the regression analysis if both are included in predicting a dependent variable.

SUMMARY

'What really makes science grow is new ideas, including false ideas' (Karl Popper, 1902–94). This famous quote from Karl Popper emphasises that the statistics play a small part in the overall scheme of a research project. The ideas, explanations and speculations discussed are just as important, if not more so, than statistical significance. The statistical significance is just giving another element of confidence with which to conclude the outcomes of your experiment. The confidence in reporting the data will be a result of your methods of controlling errors, your justification for analyses, and your justification for the level of inferential statistical significance. It will also depend on your ability to describe reliability checks, as well as the establishment and quantification of the uncertainties in the data. It should be remembered that you could never be completely certain of the truth of a hypothesis. But failure to reject an alternate hypothesis does not automatically permit acceptance of the 'null hypothesis' as being 'true'. In fact, the chance of failing to reject a false hypothesis may be rather large. It should be remembered that the option of $p < 0.05$ or $p < 0.01$ tends to be a matter of convention and therefore should be a guide rather than a rule.

10

CONSTRUCTING A DISCUSSION AND DRAWING CONCLUSIONS

LEARNING OUTCOMES

Following this chapter you should be able to:

1   structure a discussion section in an appropriate manner;
2   construct an effective argument and understand the interaction between reasoning and conclusions.

Prior to this section you should be familiar with the following terms:

*   hypothesis
*   p value.

Introduction

The final section of most dissertations or independent study projects usually consists of a discussion section. This includes a written interpretation of the results you have collected, an analysis of the methods that were used to collect the results, a discussion of previous research, and finally your conclusions. The primary purpose of the discussion is to construct an argument to support the conclusions of the study. The conclusions of a research project, as the term suggests, are traditionally positioned at the end of the piece of writing. The conclusion acts as a summary of the findings of the research and therefore should be founded on a sound base. This base comprises evidence and reasoning. The strength of the evidence is dependent on the research question and design. A good research question and design originate from a thorough understanding of the theoretical basis underlying the research area, which stems from a well-conducted literature review. The clarity of the evidence is reliant upon the correct treatment of the data, through the appropriate statistical methods, and the presentation of the data in the results section. The purpose of the discussion is to objectively interpret the evidence, to construct a line of evidence based upon this interpretation, and then assess the strength of the evidence supporting the reasoning. This process culminates in the drawing of conclusions. The entire research process can be seen as a journey starting from the development of a research question. The next step is the construction of the experimental design and an appropriate methodology. The carrying out of this methodology produces the results, which are then interpreted and conclusions drawn.

This is not a rigidly unidirectional process: sometimes results coming from a pilot study may lead to an alteration of the methods, or interpretation of some results may lead to the collection of extra data.

The discussion is a vital step in this journey. In the discussion section a researcher explicitly states their interpretation of the results and develops the reasoning which helps to generate the conclusions of the study.

Discussion and conclusion

The discussion section of any report or dissertation is crucial, as it will demonstrate your understanding of the topic. Prior to the discussion section, the writing style of the previous sections (i.e. the introduction, methods and results) has been more descriptive than analytical. The discussion section must provide a critical analysis of the results in relation to answering the question or hypotheses set. One strategy to develop in your writing is to read through the introduction and examine how you have organised your questions, aims or hypotheses. It is important that you deal with each of your hypotheses and ensure that you have fully explained what you have found and why. Common mistakes by students in their construction of the discussion section include:

1   A discussion that only describes the data and does little more than extend the results section.
2   Too little explanation of the results of the study.
3   Too much reference to other studies and a lack of comparison to the results of the study.
4   Too great an emphasis on the limitations of the study.
5   A conclusion that is not supportive of the data.
6   A conclusion that is often too strong, given the data and experimental design.

In order to score well on your assignment, the discussion should demonstrate your understanding and command of the subject. Therefore, it is important to do more than just describe the data, as this has already been performed in the results section. The reader is relying on you to communicate what has happened in order to aid their understanding of the experiment. Of course mistakes 1 and 2 mentioned above are particularly linked to the student's understanding. One of the reasons for a purely descriptive discussion is that the student does not understand the topic sufficiently to begin to explain the results. This lack of understanding can then lead to the production of mistakes 3 and 4. Hence it is easier to discuss results from other studies, rather than interpret the results of the current study. This then leads into another common mistake whereby students spend too much time concentrating on the limitations of the study, as it is often easier to criticise work than to explain the data. This can lead to the criticism that if the study has so many limitations, then it indicates you did not rigorously design your experiment in the first place!

To avoid the practice of descriptive writing in the discussion section, there are a number of strategies that you should try to employ. The first strategy is to use the opening paragraph of the discussion to confirm the aim of the study followed by a description of the key findings in your study. Note that this could include the statement that there was a small treatment effect which was neither statistically nor practically significant. In the next paragraph you should deal with the questions or hypotheses in the order that you stated them in the introduction. For each of the hypotheses and the respective results, ask the following questions:

1   Is this a worthwhile result to comment on?
2   Is it consistent with the literature and if it is different, why is it different?
3   How can you explain this result by finding support and evidence from current theories?
4   If the data do not fit a theory, are there any alternative plausible explanations?
5   Is the result worth highlighting as a possible area of future study?

After these questions have been answered in relation to each of the hypotheses, there is a choice to be made about the structure of the next paragraphs. The construction of the following paragraphs could be either a focus on the methodological limitations or the application of the results into the real world.

Methodological limitations of a study are important, particularly if there are some results that appear erroneous. Could these be due to methodological flaws? Although speculation must be used carefully in the discussion section, it should not be avoided altogether. The balance between speculation and explanation based on facts and theories is important because if too much emphasis is placed on speculative statements, it can weaken a discussion section. However, speculative statements can also demonstrate wider knowledge related to the topic.

If the methodological limitations follow an explanation of the results, it is usual to place the results in context, i.e. to discuss the practicalities of the results as they apply in the real world. Remember the p value is used as a tool to give statistical confidence in rejecting the null hypothesis, it does not say anything about the size of the effect. By reporting the practical significance alongside the statistical significance (see Chapter 9), you are demonstrating an ability to place the results in an applied setting. An understanding of the practical implications is important because much of what sport and exercise science is about is trying to enhance performance either in relation to sport, health or exercise.

Finally, once the main body of the discussion has been written, the conclusion should be constructed. This section should summarise the key points of the study carefully. Many a report or dissertation has finished weakly because a concluding paragraph was written too briefly or too verbosely. As this is the final paragraph of the work, try to finish on a positive note, by highlighting the key points rather than dwelling on the limitations. This can be achieved by concluding on the question(s) or hypotheses posed. A common mistake is that a concluding paragraph refers to all manner of variables that were not collected during the study and speculates on a number of theories that were not relevant to the project. Hence, this demonstrates that the student is unable to summarise concisely whilst synthesising the most relevant points, but instead focuses on superficial references to peripheral results.

Key points

The key points to writing the discussion and conclusion section are as follows:

1   Start by introducing what were the key findings of the study and place them in context, e.g. if this is the first time the study has been performed, then you should say so.
2   Establish the factual relationships between variables.
3   Explain the results in relation to the relevant theories.
4   Keep language simple but precise. For example, descriptors such as 'super accurate', 'fairly close', and 'quite large' are ambiguous and should be avoided.
5   Summarise the project in the final concluding paragraph positively. Concentrate on answering the question or hypotheses set and ensuring the conclusion reflects the data and does not make statements that cannot be supported by the results and experimental design.

Reasoning and conclusions

The discussion is more than just a summary of the experiment and the results; it can be thought of as an extended argument. An argument consists of premiss and conclusions. The premiss should be designed to support the conclusions. In order to do this, the premiss should have relevance and adequacy. Take the following example:

> *Premiss:* Footballers have a higher trunk strength than athletes from other sports.
> *Conclusion 1:* Therefore aerobic fitness is influential in reducing the risk of heart disease.
> *Conclusion 2:* Therefore footballers should concentrate more on psychological skills training.
> *Conclusion 3:* Therefore trunk muscle strength must be important for the twisting and turning motions occurring during playing football.

In this example conclusion 1 is not relevant to the premiss provided: heart disease risk and footballers' trunk strength are unrelated. Conclusion 2 relates to the same area of interest, but lacks adequacy. There is no logical link between the premiss and conclusion 2. The premiss has both relevance and adequacy for conclusion 3. Although, we may question the strength of the evidence provided by the premiss, in relation to conclusion 3, at least there is a logical link between the premiss and conclusion 3. The first basic step in constructing an argument is ensuring that each premiss, or piece of evidence you use, has relevance and adequacy for the conclusion you draw.

Multiple premiss and intermediate conclusions

Multiple premiss may be used to support a conclusion. For example:

> *Premiss 1:* Footballers have higher trunk strengths than athletes from other sports.

Premiss 2: EMG data have shown that twisting and turning recruits the trunk muscles.
Premiss 3: Football training improves trunk strength over time.
Conclusion: Therefore trunk muscle strength must be important for the twisting and turning motions occurring during playing football.

One of the advantages of using multiple premiss to support a conclusion is that it begins to have a summative effect. The premiss combine to increase the evidence supporting the conclusion. Additionally if one of the premiss is undermined, for example premiss 2 is rejected because of doubts about the precision of EMG measurements taken during dynamic activities, the conclusion is still underpinned by two other premiss. This is not to say that the more premiss that are used, the better. Each premiss must have relevance and adequacy and you should make assessments about the strength of the evidence relating to each premiss.

Often an intermediate conclusion is drawn, upon which the main conclusion is based, for instance:

Premiss 1: Footballers have higher trunk strengths than athletes from other sports.
Premiss 2: EMG data has shown that twisting and turning recruits the trunk muscles.
Premiss 3: Football training improves trunk strength over time.
Intermediate conclusion: Therefore trunk muscle strength must be important for the twisting and turning motions occurring during playing football.
Main conclusion: Thus, all footballers should train their trunk muscles in order to improve performance.

This is frequently used as an argument structure. One factor that you must remain constantly vigilant for is the presence of assumption. In the above example, there are parts missing to the argument that we are not given information about. How do we know that improved trunk strength will improve performance, or that this would benefit all players? The answer, in this argument, is that we don't; as a reader we are being asked to make an assumption.

Look at the following example in contrast to the previous one:

Premiss 1: Footballers have higher trunk strengths than athletes in other sports.
Premiss 2: EMG data have shown that twisting and turning recruits the trunk muscles.
Premiss 3: Football training improves trunk strength over time.
Intermediate conclusion: Therefore trunk muscle strength must be important for the twisting and turning motions occurring during playing football.
Premiss 4: Improving trunk muscle strength has been shown to improve football performance in all players.
Main conclusion: Thus, all footballers should train their trunk muscles in order to improve performance.

In this instance premiss 4 combines with the intermediate conclusion to support the main conclusion more effectively and removes some of those assumptions we were previously asked to make. The premiss that you use to support your conclusions can be drawn from one of two sources. They can come from either your own results or from other research. One of the weaknesses with being over-reliant on evidence from other research is that it lacks external validity. This means that the results found in one study may not be wholly applicable to your study. It is possible that they were collected under different conditions, in different subjects, using different equipment.

Common mistakes

1   Circular arguments, where a conclusion is repeated in slightly different forms, without any additional reasoning being added.
2   Too many assumptions, with students trying to progress an argument too quickly, without taking the time to fill in the gaps for the reader.
3   A monochrome approach to conclusion drawing. For example, 'The fatigue occurred in the absence of the accumulation of blood lactate, therefore fatigue must have been caused by dehydration.' Through only considering a restricted number of options, a student is exposing the lack of breadth to their knowledge.

SUMMARY

The discussion is generally the section of the dissertation that separates the good student from the merely competent. The process of conducting a literature review, writing a methods section and displaying the results can be quite mechanical. The discussion is an opportunity for you to display some of the critical thinking skills that are required for the top grades at this stage of your degree.

REFERENCES

Borg, W. R. and Gall, M. D. (1989) *Educational Research. An Introduction*, 5th edition. New York: Longman.

Coakes, S. J. and Steed, L. G. (2001) *SPSS: Analysis without Anguish* (Version 10.0 for Windows). Milton, Qld: Jacaranda Wiley.

Cohen, J. (1988) *Statistical Power Analysis for the Behavioral Sciences*. Hillsdale, NJ: L. Erlbaum Associates.

Hopkins, W. G. (2000) 'Measures of reliability in sports medicine and science', *Sports Medicine*, 30(1): 1–15.

Hopkins, W. G., Hawley, J. A. and Burke, L. M. (1999) 'Design and analysis of research on sport performance enhancement', *Medicine and Science in Sports and Exercise*, 31(3): 472–85.

Kadaba, M. P., Wootten, M. E., Gainey, J. and Cochran, G. V. (1985) 'Repeatability of phasic muscle activity performance of surface and intramuscular wire electrodes in gait analysis', *Journal of Orthopaedic Research*, 3(3): 350–9.

Kerlinger, F. N. (1986) *Foundations of Behavioral Research*, 3rd edn. New York: Holt, Rinehart & Winston.

Thomas J. R. and Nelson, J. K. (1990) *Research Methods in Physical Activity*, 2nd edition. Champaign, IL: Human Kinetics.

Wonnacott, T. (1987) 'Confidence intervals or hypothesis tests?', *Journal of Applied Statistics*, 14(3): 195–201.

INDEX

Al-Khwarizmi, Abu Ja'far Muhammad ibn Musa 3
alternate hypothesis 61, 64, 65, 66, 72, 83, 95
ANOVA: assumptions 72, 73, 95; equations 72; F score 72; Kruskal-Wallis ANOVA 94, 95, 100; one-way repeated measures 73; simple one-way analysis 72–3; Statistical Package for the Social Sciences (SPSS) 73; two-way 75
Arabic civilisation 3
Aristotle 1, 2, 3, 5
Armstrong, Neil 7–8
assumptions: ANOVA 72, 73, 95; bivariate regression 87; chi-squares 99–100; correlations 87; multiple regression 90; non-parametric tests 95; sphericity 73; t tests 68–9, 70
averages: group comparisons 48, 59; individual comparisons 47–8; mean see mean; meaning 47; median see median; mode see mode; types 48–9
axioms 3, 4

Bacon, Francis 3–4, 5
bar charts 105, 106
bias 57, 99
Biddle, Stuart 8
bimodal distribution 53
bivariate regression: assumptions 87; line of best fit 85–6, 87, 88; relationship 85–9
black crow hypothesis 6
Byzantium 3

case studies 37
causality: causal-comparative design 43; cause and effect 43–4, 117–18, 121; correlational design 43–4; third variables 43; true experiment 40
Cavanagh, Peter 8
cell theory 5–6
chance: chi-square values 99; correlations 83; differences 63, 64, 67, 68

chemistry 3, 5
chi-squares 98–100
coefficient: coefficient of determination 84, 118; multiple determination 89; product moment correlation coefficient 82–4, 98; rank order correlation coefficient 97–8, 100; variation (CV) 57
Cohen, Jacob 115, 118
collinearity 90, 123
common mistakes: correlations 121; difference 75; discussion 125, 126, 129; experimental design 29; literature review 26, 28; non-parametric statistics 100; presentation of data 103, 111–12; relationship 91
common sense 50, 114, 123
common variance: quantification 84, 118; standard deviation 80
communication 101, 108, 114, 125
comparisons: causal-comparative design 43; familywise error 71–2, 75; groups 48, 59; individuals 47–8; multiple 71
conclusions 124–9
constancy 37
construct validity 34
control groups: crossing over 42; demoralisation 40; external validity 39; internal validity 31–2
Copernican system 4
correlation coefficient: equations 82; outliers 121; prediction 122; product moment 82–4, 98; rank order 97–8, 100; size 84
correlations: assumptions 87; cause and effect 43–4, 117–18, 121; chance 83; common mistakes 121; correlational design 43–4; dependent variables 84; independent variables 84; interpretation 84–5, 117–21; negative values 82, 83, 85, 86; positive values 82, 83, 86; psychology 118; range of data 118–20; relationship 82–5, 118; size 18, 118; statistical significance 83, 118, 120–1;